THE NEGRO STILL IS NOT FREE

Askari Hesabu

THE NEGRO STILL IS NOT FREE
ASKARI HESABU

https://www.facebook.com/busybeepublication/
Serving all of your publishing needs

Published in the United States

CONTENTS

Acknowledgment

First and foremost, I want to give all praises to the creator, Amen.

Special thanks to Mrs. Connie and Busybee Publications who assured that my book was published.

High honor to my cultural father, guide and mentor, Mr. Richard "MuFundi" Lake, who went back to the ancestors on January 21, 2018-UHURU!

I want to thank my family and friends for their support. Special thanks to all the freedom fighters and educators, who teach the masses about the incarceration of the black and brown masses: Michelle Alexandra, Dr. Umar Johnson, Rahiem Shabazz, Owne "Alik" Shahadah and everyone who's doing their duty as a "civilizer" – HOTEP! To everyone who supports the Free Alabama Movement. To my Brothers: Bennu Hannibal Ra-Sun, Kinetic Justice, Rah'mel Amma, Asil. Tufe Amun, Fahamiza Amun-HOTEP! To the Queen Karma Binah. Love and honor.

To my family, Graig and the entire 313 "Black Michigan" FAMILY. FREE THE FAMILY!

To everyone not named but still is a part of this struggle – ONE!

Introduction

One of the essential goals of slave owners was to ensure that slaves did not communicate with other men or women of their native tongue. They (slave owners) purposely separated tribal members to prevent insurrections and possible takeovers of slave ships and plantations.

Unity amongst Afrikans was somewhat of a phobia for white slave owners, and to see two or more Afrikans congregated was deemed as a threat to their white supremacist control, which they knew would not last forever.

I

Willie Lynch Letter

December 25, 1712

Gentlemen:

I greet you here on the bank of the James River in the year of our Lord one thousand seven hundred and twelve. First, I shall thank you, the gentlemen of the Colony of Virginia, for bringing me here. I am here to help you solve some of your problems with slaves. Your invitation reached me on my modest plantation in the West Indies, where I have experimented with some of the newest and still the oldest methods for control of slaves. Ancient Rome's would envy us if my program is implemented.

As our boat sailed south on the James River, named for our illustrious King, whose version of the Bible we cherish, I saw enough to know that your problem is not unique. While Rome used cords of wood as crosses for standing human bodies along its highways in great numbers, you are here using the tree and the rope on occasions. I caught the whiff of a dead slave hanging from a tree, a couple miles back. You are not only losing valuable stock by hangings, you are having uprisings, slaves are running away, your crops are sometimes left in the fields too long for maximum profit, you suffer occasional fires, your animals are killed.

Gentlemen, you know what your problems are; I do not need to elaborate. I am not here to enumerate your problems, I am here to introduce you to a method of solving them. In my bag here, *I have a full proof method for controlling your black slaves.* I guarantee every one of you that if installed correctly, *it will control the slaves for at least 300 years.* My method is simple. Any member of your family or your overseer can use it. *I have outlined a number of differences among the slaves and make the differences bigger. I use fear, distrust, and envy for control purposes.*

These methods have worked on my modest plantation in the West Indies and it will work throughout the South.

Take this simple little list of differences and think about them. On top of my list is "age" but it's there only because it starts with an "A."

The second is "COLOR" or shade, there is **intelligence, size, sex, size of plantations and status** on plantations, **attitude** of owners, whether the slaves live in the valley, on a hill, East, West, North, South, have fine hair, coarse hair, or is tall or short. Now that you have a list of differences, I shall give you an outline of action, but before that, I shall assure you that **distrust is stronger than trust and envy stronger than adulation, respect or admiration**. The Black slaves after receiving this indoctrination shall carry on and will become self-refueling and self-generating for **hundreds of years**, maybe thousands. Don't forget you must pitch the **OLD** black Male vs. the **YOUNG** black Male, and the young black Male against the old black male. You must use the **DARK** skin slaves vs. the **LIGHT** skin slaves, and the **LIGHT** skin slaves vs. the **DARK** skin slaves. You must use the female vs. the male. And the male vs. the female. You must also have you white servants and overseers distrust all Blacks. It is *necessary that your slaves trust and depend on us. They must love, respect and trust only us.* Gentlemen, these kits are your keys to control. Use them. Have your wives and children use them, never miss an opportunity. *If used intensely for one year, the slaves themselves will remain perpetually distrustful of each other.*

(Additional Note: "Henry Berry, speaking in the Virginia House of Delegates in 1832, described the situation as it existed in many parts of the South at this time: "We have, as far as possible, closed every avenue by which light may enter their (the slaves) minds. If we could extinguish the capacity to see the light, our work would be complete, they would then be on a level with the beasts of the field and we should be safe. I am not certain that we would not do it if we could find out the process and that on the plea of necessity." From Brown America, The story of a New Race by Edwin

Thank you gentlemen
(R. Embree., 1931 The Viking Press.)

LET'S MAKE A SLAVE

It was the interest and business of slaveholders to study human nature, and the slave nature in particular, with a view to practical results. I and many of them attained astonishing proficiency in this direction. They had to deal not with earth, wood, and stone, but with men and by every regard, they had for their own safety and prosperity they needed to know the material on which they were to work. Conscious of the injustice and wrong they were every hour perpetuating and knowing what they themselves would do. Were they the victims of such wrongs? They were constantly looking for the first signs of the dreaded retribution. They watched, therefore with skilled and practiced eyes, and learned to read with great accuracy, the state of mind and heart of the slave, through his sable face. Unusual sobriety, apparent abstractions, sullenness and indifference indeed, any mood out of the common was afforded ground for suspicion and inquiry.

Frederick Douglas:

Let us make a slave is a sturdy of scientific process of man breaking and slave making. It describes the rationale and results of the Anglo Saxon' ideas and methods of ensuring the master/slave relationship. "LET'S MAKE A SLAVE" The Original and Development of a Social Being Called "The Negro." Let us make a slave.

What do we need? First of all, we need a black *n-word* man, a pregnant *n-word* woman, and her baby *n-word* boy. Second, we will use the same basic principle that we use in breaking a horse, combined with some more sustaining factors. What we do with horses is that we break them from one form of life to another, that is, we reduce them from their natural state in nature. Whereas nature provides them with the natural capacity to take care of their offspring, we break that natural string of independence from them and thereby create a dependency status, so that we may be able to get from them useful production for our business and pleasure.

CARDINAL PRINCIPLES FOR MAKING A NEGRO

For fear that our future Generations may not understand the principles of breaking both of the beasts together, the *n-word* and the horse. We understand that short range planning economics results in periodic economic, particular attention must be paid to the **FEMALE** and the **YOUNGEST** offspring. Both must be **CROSSBRED** to produce a variety and division of labor. Both must be taught to respond to a peculiar new **LANGUAGE**. Psychological and physical instruction of **CONTAINMENT** must be created for both. We hold the six cardinal principles as truth to be self-evident, based upon the following the discourse concerning the economics of breaking and tying the horse and the *n-word* together, all inclusive of the six principles laid down about.

NOTE: Neither principle alone will suffice for good economics. All principles must be employed for the orderly good of the nation. Accordingly, both a wild horse and a wild or nature *n-word* is dangerous even if captured, for they will have the tendency to seek their customary freedom, and in doing so, might kill you in your sleep. You cannot rest. They sleep while you are awake, and are awake while you are asleep. They are **DANGEROUS** near the family house and it requires too much labor to watch them away from the house. Above all, you cannot get them to work in this natural state. Hence both the horse and the *n-word* must be broken; that is breaking them from one form of mental life to another. **KEEP THE BODY TAKE THE MIND!** In other words, break the will to resist. Now the breaking process is the same for both the horse and the *n-word*, only slightly varying in degrees.

But as we said before, there is an art in long-range economic planning. *You must keep your eye and thoughts on the female and the offspring* of the horse and the *n-word*. A brief discourse in offspring development will shed light on the key to sound economic principles. Pay little attention to the generation of original breaking, but *concentrate on future generations.*

Therefore, if you break the **FEMALE** mother, she will **BREAK** the offspring in its early years of development and when the offspring is old enough to work, she will deliver it up to you, for her normal female protective tendencies will have been lost in the original breaking process. For example, take the case of the wild stud horse, a female horse, and an already infant horse and compare the breaking process with two captured *n-word* males in their natural state, a pregnant *n-word* woman with her infant offspring. Take the stud horse, break him for limited containment.

Completely break the female horse until she becomes very gentle, whereas you or anybody can ride her in her comfort.

Breed the mare and the stud until you have the desired offspring. Then you can turn the stud to freedom until you need him again. Train the female horse whereby she will eat out of your hand, and she will in turn train the infant horse to eat out of your hand also. When it comes to breaking the uncivilized *n-word*, use the same process, but vary the degree and step up the pressure, so as to do a complete reversal of the mind. Take the meanest and most restless *n-word*, strip him of his clothes in front of the remaining male *n-words*, the female, and the *n-word* infant, tar and feather him, tie each leg to a different horse faced in opposite directions, set him afire and beat both horses to pull him apart in front of the remaining *n-words*. The next step is to take a bull whip and beat the remaining *n-word* male to the point of death, in front of the female and the infant. Don't kill him, but **PUT THE FEAR OF GOD IN HIM**, for he can be useful for future breeding.

THE BREAKING PROCESS OF THE AFRICAN WOMAN

Take the female and run a series of tests on her to see if she will submit to your desires willingly. Test her in every way, because she is the most important factor for good economics. If she shows any sign of resistance in submitting completely to your will, do not hesitate to use the bull whip on her to extract that last bit of resistance out of her. Take care not to kill her, for in doing so, you spoil good economics. When in complete submission, she will train her offsprings in the early years to submit to labor when they become of age.

Understanding is the best thing. Therefore, we shall go deeper into this area of the subject matter concerning what we have produced here in this breaking process of the female *n-word*. We have reversed the relationship in her natural uncivilized state she would have a strong dependency on the uncivilized *n-word* male, and she would have a limited protective tendency toward her independent male offspring and would raise male offsprings to be dependent like her. Nature had provided for this type of balance. We reversed nature by burning and pulling a civilized *n-word* apart and bull whipping the other to the point of death, all in her presence. By her being left alone, unprotected, with the **MALE IMAGE DESTROYED,** the ordeal caused her to move from her psychological dependent state to a frozen independent state. In this frozen psychological state of independence, she will raise her **MALE** and female offspring in reversed roles.

For **FEAR** of the young male's life, she will psychologically train him to be **MENTALLY WEAK AND DEPENDENT**, but physically strong. Because she has become psychologically independent, she will train her female offsprings to be psychological independent. What have you got? You've got the *n-word women out front and the n-word man behind and scared.* This is a perfect situation of sound sleep and economic. Before the breaking process, we had to be alertly on guard at all times.[i]

Now we can sleep soundly, for out of frozen fear his woman stands guard for us. He cannot get past her early slave molding process. He is a good tool, now ready to be tied to the horse at a tender age. By the time an *n-word* boy reaches the age of sixteen, he is soundly broken in and ready for a long life of sound and efficient work and the reproduction of a unit of good labor force. Continually through the breaking of uncivilized savage *n-word*, by throwing the *n-word* female savage into a frozen psychological state of independence, by killing of the protective male image, and by creating a submissive dependent mind of the *n-word* male slave, we have created an orbiting cycle that turns on its own axis forever, unless a phenomenon occurs and re-shifts the position of the male and female slaves. We show what we mean by example. Take the case of the two economic slave units and examine them closely.

THE NEGRO WORD MARRIAGE UNIT

We breed two *n-word* males with two *n-word* females. Then we take the *n-word* males away from them and keep them moving and working. Say one *n-word* female bears an *n-word* female and the other bears an *n-word* male. Both *n-word* females being without influence of the *n-word* male image, frozen with an independent psychology, will raise their offspring into reverse positions. The one with the female offspring will teach her to be like herself, independent and negotiable (we negotiate with her, through her, by her, we negotiate her at will). The one with the *n-word* male offspring, she being frozen with a subconscious fear for his life, will raise him to be mentally dependent and weak, but **PHYSICALLY STRONG**, in other words, body over mind. Now in a few years when these two offspring's become fertile for early reproduction, we will mate and breed them and continue the cycle. That is good, sound, and long range comprehensive planning.

WARNING: POSSIBLE INTERLOPING NEGATIVES

Earlier we talked about the noneconomic good of the horse and the *n-word* in their wild or natural state; we talked out the principle of breaking and tying them together for orderly production. Furthermore, we talked about paying particular attention to the female savage and her offspring for orderly future planning, then more recently we stated that, by reversing the positions of the male and female savages, we created an orbiting cycle that turns on its own axis forever unless a phenomenon occurred and resift and positions of the male and female savages. Our experts warned us about the possibility of this phenomenon occurring, for they say that the mind has a strong drive to correct and re-correct itself over a period of time if I can touch some substantial original historical base, and they advised us that the best way to deal with the phenomenon is to shave off the brute's mental history and create a multiplicity of phenomena of illusions, so that each illusion will twirl in its own orbit, something similar to floating balls in a vacuum.

This creation of a multiplicity of phenomena of illusions entails the principle of crossbreeding the *n-word* and the horse as we stated above, the purpose of which is to create a diversified division of labor thereby creating different levels of labor and different values of illusion at each connecting level of labor. The results of which is the severance of the points of original beginnings for each sphere illusion. Since we feel that the subject matter may get more complicated as we proceed in laying down our economic plan concerning the purpose, reason, and effect of crossbreeding horses and *n-word*, we shall lay down the following definition terms for future generations.

Orbiting cycle means a thing turning in a given path. Axis means upon which or around which a body turns. Phenomenon means something beyond ordinary conception and inspires awe and wonder. Multiplicity means a great number. Sphere means a globe. Cross breeding a horse means taking a horse and breeding it with an ass and you get a dumb backward ass long headed mule that is not reproductive nor productive by itself.

Crossbreeding *n-words* mean taking so many drops of good white blood and putting them into as many *n-word* women as possible, varying the drops by the various tone that you want, and then letting them breed with each other until another cycle of color appears as you desire. What this means is this; put the *n-words* and the horse in a breeding pot, mix some assess and some good white blood and what do you get? You got a multiplicity of colors of ass backward, unusual *n-words*, running, tied to a backward ass long headed mule, the one productive of itself, the other sterile. (The one constant, the other dying, we keep the *n-word* constant for we may replace the mules for another tool) both mule and *n-word* tied to each other, neither knowing where the other came from and neither productive for itself nor without each other.

CONTROL THE LANGUAGE

Crossbreeding completed, for further severance from their original beginning, we must completely annihilate the mother tongue of both the new *n-word* and the new mule and institute a new language that involves the new life's work of both.

You know language is a peculiar institution. It leads to the heart of a people. The more a foreigner knows about the language of another country the more he is able to move through all levels of that society. Therefore, if the foreigner is an enemy of the country, to the extent that he knows the body of the language, to that extent is the country vulnerable to attack or invasion of a foreign culture. For example, if you take a slave, if you teach him all about your language, he will know all your secrets, and he is then no more a slave, for you can't fool him any longer. For example, if you told a slave that he must perform in getting out "our crops" and he knows the language well, he would know that "our crops" didn't mean "our crops" and the slavery system would break down, for he would relate on the basis of what "our crops" really meant. So you have to be careful in setting up the new language for the slaves would soon be in your house, talking to you "man to man" and that is death to our economic system. In addition, the definitions of words or terms are only a minute part of the process. Values are created and transported by communication through the body of the language. A total society has many interconnected value system. All the values in the society have bridges of language to connect them for orderly working in the society. But for these language bridges, these many value systems would sharply clash and cause internal strife or civil war, the degree of the conflict being determined by the magnitude of the issues or relative opposing strength in whatever form.

For example, if you put a slave in a hog pen and train him to live there and incorporate in him to value it as a way of life completely, the biggest problem you would have out of him is that he would worry you about provisions to keep the hog pen clean, or the same hog pen and make a slip and incorporate something in his language whereby he comes to value a house more than he does his hog pen, you got a problem. He will soon be in your house.[ii]

II

THE LETTER

In the spring of 1712, a West Indies slave owner named William (Willie) Lynch gave an abhorrent speech on the banks of the James River in Virginia. Lynch's speech was an in-depth illustration of the methods of making the ideal slave. His program was based on the concepts and principles of an old, but well-known mind controlling doctrine called MENTICIDE, which consists of four main systems: 1) FEAR,   2) INFERIOR, OFFSPRING BREEDING 3)SEPARATION, 4) INDOCTRINATION.

In his speech, Lynch, assured his audience, that in his bag he contained "A foolproof method for controlling your Black slave", and he guaranteed everyone that "If installed correctly, it will control the slaves for at least 300 years".

Lynch's' first instruction was to take the numerous differences amongst the slaves and make them bigger. He asserted that this would be capable by implementing jealousy, envy, distrust, and fear amongst the slaves. These purposeful tools would become the fundamental principles of the disenfranchisement of the entire Afrikan population in the wilderness of North America. Once these principles were implemented, strife and conflicts between Afrikans became more common.

As was seen in previous times, whenever Caucasian white people spread lies and cause mischief amongst the original people; it causes them to fight and kill one another. This system of DIVIDE AND CONQUER was an essential component in the making of the perfect slave, a slave that would be more loyal and trustworthy to his "MASSA" than he would be towards his own people. A slave that will be self-refueling and self-generating for hundreds, perhaps thousands of years. This new slave would become known as the NIGGER.

A: The Systematic Physical Breaking and Psychological Reversing Progress Fear

In this part of Lynch's speech, he gave a graphic illustration of how to "Break a slave's will to resist". He compared the breaking of an Afrikan, to the breaking of a "MULE" with the degree of affliction varying slightly. Lynch saw all Afrikan people the same way he viewed any domesticated livestock, and therefore their lives were expendable.

Needless to say, that Lynch's' system of breaking a slave's will, was far beyond the bounds of inhumanity and extremely satanic. Lynch focal point wasn't directly aimed at the generation of slaves at hand, but rather at the future generation of predictable slaves.

To maintain his system, Lynch stressed the importance of the Afrikan female slave and the need for 'Careful Selection'. He knew, that in order to produce a breed of the most desirable offspring, A METHOD OF "Control Mating" must be precisely implemented. This scientific field of Eugenics, along with *fear* would be the vehicle in which the idea slave would be made.

The "varying of affliction" mention earlier in this text is an understatement, considering the facts that millions of Afrikans lost their lives in some of the most horrifying ways. In a contradictory statement, Lynch insisted that death was not always necessary, considering the fact that the slave was "valuable stock" but then recommended that slave-owners should:

> Take the meanest and most restless nigger, strip him of his clothes in front of the remaining male niggers, the female and the infant nigger; tar and feather him, tie each arm to a different horse faced in opposite directions, set him afire, and beat both horses to pull him apart in front of the remaining niggers. The next step is to take a bull whip and beat the remaining nigger male to the point of death in front of the female and her infant. Don't kill him, but put the fear of God in him, for he can be useful for future breeding.

B: The Breaking Process Inferior Offspring Breeding

Breeding: is a method of changing or maintain a kind of animal, plant, or in this case, a human by careful selection of parents. One method of breeding involves mating the most desirable offspring or kind for a **DEFINITE PURPOSE,** such as producing speed, height, endurance, or "a slave that will be mentally dependent and weak, but physically strong". The breeding of

special strains of organisms for the purpose of enhancing desired traits is a unique and continuous process. Traits are determined by genes, the instruction encoded in the DNA (Deoxyribonucleic acid) of the chromosomes an individual receives from each parent. Parents do not transmit traits directly to their offspring, rather they pass on units of information that operate in the offspring to produce the trait. This is called "factors" or in scientific terminology "genes".

A gene is a segment of a DNA molecule that transmits hereditary information. For each trait, the individual has two factors, one from its mother and one from its father.

Knowing this, Lynch degree to his audience of Virginians was to take the female slave and try to seduce her in every manner to submit willingly to their desires. He reminded them that, the Black female slave is the most important factor. However, if she shows any sign of resistance, do not hesitate to use the bullwhip to "extract the last bit of bitch out of her". This not only breaks the female will to rebuff but also cause her to be overtaken by fear and anxiety.

Fear, as noted earlier, was the principal element and objective of the entire slave making system. Although fear is defined as an emotion, a psychological and behavioral response to a recognized external threat, it was the psychological and psychogenic aspect of it in which Lynch's' system focused on. A campaign directed at abolishing Afrikans morale and debasing them to the pit of **Chattel**. Fear from a psychological aspect can cause an individual to become mentally unstable by offsetting the chemical balance of the brain.

Homeostasis is a state of equilibrium in which the internal environment of the body remains in the normal range. When such dangers are sensed, nerve impulses are directed to the hypothalamus (a portion of the brain located below the thalamus and forming the floor of the third ventricle) triggering physiological responses that resist a loss of homeostasis. These responses often include increased activity in the sympathetic division of the atomic nerve system and increased secretion of adrenal hormones. The factor that stimulated this response is called **Stressor** and the condition it produces in the body is called **Stress**. Stressors may be physical, psychological, or both. Physical stress threatens the nervous system and can damage vital tissue if continued for long periods of time. A person suffering from this type of stress condition can develop stomach ulcers, hypertension, cardiac diseases, and thrombosis. Psychological stress deal strictly with the mental stability of the mind. This type of stress may cause a person to become schizophrenic, paranoid, depress, and suffer from any of the numerous anxiety disorders, such as... hypochondria and posttraumatic stress.

In order to "Make a Slave," each cardinal principles must be applied or neither principle alone would suffice to produce the most desirable offspring – "The Nigger". The scientific process of slave-making is simple by nature, the creating, enhancing and maintaining a **Black inferiority – White superiority** gene or trait that would be passed down from one generation of slaves to the next. With this determined idea, Lynch based his system upon genetic engineering and the scientific field of eugenics. Genetic engineering is the manipulation of DNA to modify hereditary features, eugenics; is the measure (the manipulation of DNA) intended to improve the qualities of a human population, by such means as discouraging or encouraging inheritable traits.

As delineated earlier, Lynch instructed his audience to take a male slave and mutilate his body in front of a pregnant female slave, a child, and another male slave; then beat the remaining male slaves to the point of near death. This takes the protective dependency away from the female slave and leaves here in a frozen independent state. With fear embedded within her mental and physical being, the female slave becomes vulnerable, submissive, and a tool used by slave owners to control the male and her offspring. This process reverses the natural order of the male – female relationship. Seeing the male figure broken to the point of *chattel*, she becomes the dominant figure in the household, thereby teaching and training her male offspring to be inferior, submissive, and mentally weak and dependent, but physically strong enough to endure a long life of slavery. She will teach her female offspring to be like herself, in a frozen psychologically independent state; and her husband to be submissive and dependent upon their slave owner in order to stay alive and keep the family together.

It was through this process that slaves were being made in the womb of their mothers, and from birth, they were taught the fundamentals of slave life. Lynch stated "by throwing the nigger female savage into a frozen psychological state of independence, *by killing of the protective male image, and by creating a submissive dependent mind of the nigger male slave, we have created an orbiting cycle that turns of its own axis forever,* ("unless a phenomenon occurs and re-shirts that position of the male and female slave").

This slave making system, the rationale, and results of the Anglo-Saxons', their ideas and methods of ensuring the Master/slave relationship, a scientific process that closed every avenue by which light (Knowledge of Self) may enter into a slaves' mind.

C: The Negro Marriage Unit Separation Page

Slavery, by Americas' recollection, is a fait accompli (**a thing that has been done and is irreversible**). There will never exist, an instrument that could gauge the degree of detrimental effects(s), (psychological, physical, social, economical, educational, political etc...etc...), that this unprecedented system has burden Afrikan people with. And it is precise to say that, the Nigger is a by-product of America; just as Negro is to Europe. To fully understand this system and how it affects its Afrikan subjects in so many different ways, we must view the continuity of the "orbiting cycle" of this man breaking, slave-making machine.

When expounding on the scientific process of control-mating, Lynch's first rule was to make sure that all the slaves were healthy, strong, and good breeders. If not, he sent them back (the slaves that were not good in multiplying), and the ones that were; should marry at the age of sixteen. In order for a male and female slave to marry, they must first be qualified by their slave owner. Slaves that were deemed "undesirable or rebellious" in nature, could not marry nor mate. Only those that were submissive and broken could be married and reproduce.

Next, Lynch instructed that they should take the male slaves away from their families, and keep them moving and working, leaving only the female slaves at home to rear their children and take care of the duties of the household. Being left alone, unprotected, with the *male image destroyed* and *in a frozen state*, these Afrikan male counterparts, financially dependent on their Caucasian white…slave masters. Although families were sometimes kept tougher for breeding purposes, female slaves often lost respect and honor for their husbands and no longer saw them as men of dignity and pride. This made it easier for slave owners to further disunify their Afrikan subjects, disband family structure; and implement a principle that Lynch termed – *Cross-breeding*.

Lynch law on *Cross-breeding* (to be enforced while making a slave), was to "take so many drops of good white blood and put them into as many nigger women as possible", destroy the alike and save the unlike which means kill the (black babies) and save the brown babies, then let them breed with each other until circle of colors appeared as you desire. Lynch, with his law on Cross-breeding - inculcated to inseminate a more recessive germ into the Black female, thus, by thinning the original blood making it weak, wicked and half original, and no more the same, slave owners were able to destroy the Black dominate germ, and produce mulatto slave children. With this principle enacted, disunity reached its apex.

In his introduction, Lynch stated that he had a list of the numerous differences among slaves that slave-makers should use and enhance in order to advance the disunsification between slaves. The first of his list of differences was AGE, then color. Although Lynch insisted that age was the top of his list merely because it begin with letter "A", it was at this phase of his system, that the history and conventional wisdom that was once passed down by the elders was extirpated. The more slave-makers incited strike, lies, envy, and distrustfulness between subjugated Afrikans, the bigger and wider the generational gap became.

Next on this list was color. To achieve this, Lynch vented his laws and instruction on Cross-breeding to his audience. Which in actuality was a decree to barbarically rape and sodomize Afrikan women, and to unmercifully kill all predominant complexion infants. These differences, along with others, gave rise to a "**Plantation Caste System**" that has lasted longer than slavery itself.

Many have asked the question, *"What was the difference in slavery before and after the instituting of the William Lynch slave-making system?"*

Slavery, before the introduction of the Willie Lynch's system, was obtainable mostly by forcible tactics… Note:

> The first Afrikan captives to arrive in the wilderness of North America was aboard a slave ship commanded by an English slave trader named Sir John Hawkins, in the year 1555. According to Americas' History test; the Afrikan slave trade was established 64 years later, in the year that the slave trade became commercialized and an industry which involved numerous businesses, shipping companies, Kings and Queens, and many religious clergymen such as People and Bishops of the church.

For the first 157 years of slavery, there were many slave revolts, uprisings, and countless escapes. Although there were trading posts in the jungle of Africa, there were no efficient breaking ports; until the establishments of those in the West Indies. It was there, in the Islands between southeast North American and North South America, separating the Caribbean Sea and the Atlantic, and including the Greater Antilles, the Lesser Antilles, and the Bahamas that slavery became 85% psychological, 10% religious and only 5% physical. With the introduction of the William Lynch system to North America, Afrikans became indoctrinated into the acceptance of the belief of their slavish conditions. A belief that all Afrikans (Hamites) were cursed and GOD made them slaves.

D: Indoctrination Control Language

Before Lynch continued with his lecture, he advised this audience of the possibility of the occurrence of a phenomenon which he termed "Interloping Negatives". The word interlope, according to Webster's Lexicon; means:

1. To violate the legal rights, esp., the trading rights, of others.
2. To interfere in the affairs of others.

To word negative, in align with this usage, means:

1. Opposition to thing regarded as positive: (a) such as a statement, word, viewpoint, agreement, etc.

In perceptive with the above definitions, interloping negatives would mean something beyond ordinary that could interfere; in a negative way, with the slave-master relationship, and violate the so-called *legal rights* of slave owners and traders: to abduct, enslave, kill, rape; torture and /or do whatsoever to the slave, as he/she sees fit.

In his letter, Lynch does not give an in-depth and exegesis of what this phenomenon could be. However, he does state that:

> "Our experts warned us about the possibility of this phenomenon occurring for they say that the mind (of Afrikan people) has a strong drive to correct and re-correct itself over a period of time. **If it can touch some substantial original historical base**".

It should be known that this phenomenon mention by Lynch was not the abolishment of slavery thru/or by the signing of the Emancipation Proclamation on January 1, 1863. For the very fact that southern states, particular Alabama, held Afrikans in involuntary servitude up until the early 1900's. Nor was the rights and privileges guaranteed by the Constitution of this said government because Afrikans born or naturalized in this country still have not gain, **HUMAN RIGHTS**, *which establish them as an independent nation of people*. For reasons being that the American Negro has no dutiful meaning under this constitution, nor any other; (Dred Scott Decision 1857), becomes by definition the Negro is and will always be a property of this Caucasian enslaver and colonizer.

Before I explain what this interloping negative of the phenomenon, that experts caution them about, we must first examine Lynch's final tool or principle of his system.

INDOCTRINATION

English Lesson C 1-36

1. My name is W.F. Muhhamed.
2. I came to North America by myself.
3. My uncle was brought over here by the Trader 379 years ago.
4. My uncle cannot speak his own language.
5. He does not know that he is my uncle.
6. He likes the Devil because the Devil gives him nothing.
7. Why does he like the Devil?
8. Because the Devil put fear in him when he was a little boy.
9. Why does he fear, now, since he is a big man?
10. Because the Devil taught him to eat the wrong food.
11. Does that have anything to do with the above question, # 10?
12. Yes, sir! That makes him other than his own self.

The above questionnaire is an excerpt from the **SUPREME WISDOM** Lessons, a book composed by the Honorable Elijah Muhammad. In this lesson, the initiator W.F. Muhammad has an uncle that is a captured Afrikan brought to America by a slave trader 379 years before his arrival. His uncle suffers from the Willie Lynch Syndrome. The statement made in sentence #4, states:

4) He does not speak his own language.

There's an old adage that says... "Whoever controls the languages of the people, controls the people also". The abolishment of the Afrikan dialect or native tongue, spoken by the countless number of slaves that were brought to this country; was essential to this subordinate doctrine. The lack of communication amongst slaves meant the lack of unity. From the lack of unity descends the lack of trust, and it was thru this breach, that slave-makers not only mass-produced niggers but was able to control them with little or no force at all.

Slave owners made speaking **The King's Language** seem more civilized than their own Afrikan dialect. Therefore, slaves who learned to speak proper English fluently, considered themselves better than those who could not. Slave owners only taught certain slaves to speak in this manner, preferably those considered vulnerable and easy to be manipulated. They would then make these slaves **Overseers** and **Personal slaves**, and raise their status above their Afrikan counterparts, driving the wedge of separation deeper into already deteriorating unity and widening the gap of trust amongst the slaves.

Lynch knew the importance of phonics and the extent a slave owner should teach a slave the power of the English language. Therefore, Lynch stressed to his fellow Virginians that if a slave should fully understand the power of the spoken language; controlling them as slaves would be virtually impossible.

"If you teach him (the slave) all about your language, he will know all your secrets, and he is then no more a slave, for you can't fool him any longer, and being

a fool is one of the basic ingredients of and incidents
to the maintenance of the slavery system."

This is why slave owners and Caucasians, in general, kept
Afrikans apart from their social equality. They knew that
once Afrikans found out how filthy they are and all of their
affairs that they would run from them amongst
themselves. Lynch knew that once slaves became serious
and learn the language well, that they would really know
that "our crop" don't really mean theirs and the **"Massa"**.
And that it would be at that point that the respect and value
placed on their owners; property would quickly decay,
along with the respect for the Massa. Lynch warned them
that if they allow the slave to break down the barrier of
autocracy that "soon the slave would be in their houses
talking to them MAN TO MAN".

5) He does not know that he is my uncle.

The overall objective of the Willie Lynch's system was to
make the Afrikan subjects value being slaves. As the
indoctrination of slavery deepened within the slaves'
psyche, and as the generational system continued; slaves
grew farther apart from their Afrikan roots. Despite the
fact that 98% of slaves brought to the Americas were
abducted from the West and West-central coastal region
of Africa; and many from the same tribes. The third and
fourth generation of Lynch's system couldn't related to
the close family ties of newly arriving Afrikan slaves.

**6) He likes the Devil because the Devil gives him
nothing.**

To convert a nation of people away from their God, their heritage and history away from their ancestral beliefs, language and culture, a science so artful must be subliminally imposed which eradicates all previous knowledge of whom and what they were before. Then they must be reinter-orientated with an entirely new and different knowledge of self. A knowledge that will make them unalike to the very nature in which they were born.

7) Why does he like the Devil?

> **Indoctrination** (in-dok' tren-nat') tr.v. –nat – ed, -nat-ing, -nati-ion. 1. To instruct in a body of doctrine. 2) to teach to accept a system of thought uncritically.

Ever hear of the cliché, "*Sticks and stones may break my bones, but words will never hurt*". Well when it comes to the doctrine of **Menticide**, words are as harmful as sticks and stones.

Menticide (ment-i-cide). The systematic effort to undermine and destroy a person's values, principles, and beliefs, as by the use of prolonged interrogation, torture, drugs, etc… and to induce radically different ideas.

8) Because the Devil planted fear in him when he was a little boy.

Slavery, "Systematic slavery", defined by America and the West Indies; was 85% mental, 10% spiritual, and 5% physical.

Before reaching North America, 95% of slaves abducted from Afrikan were shipped to **Breading Ports** in the West

Indies. It was these Isles that codified the notorious **Transatlantic Triangular Slave Trade.** In these inhumane prison camps, countless men, women, and children were brutally beaten, starved, raped; harassed, and tortured repeatedly onto a submissive state of being called **Broken**.

It was by this process that slave makers were able to as humanize their Afrikan subjects to a state of live chattel, and almost completely obliterated the vast cultural history of Africa and its people. Not only were these newly acquired human merchandise forced by penalty of death to abandon everything they once knew and believed in and to accept their now perpetual life of bondage. They also had to be **civilized** before they could be auction off to a potential buyer. Once a slave was labeled "broke", they would then be passed on to a doctor, who would, in turn, examine them for any type of illness, disease or physical defeats. The doctor would then qualify or disqualify them to the minister. The minister would then baptize those qualified by the doctor as Christians, and interpret certain scriptures or quotes in a way that would make the slaves believe, that the reason they're in bondage is because "Black People" was cursed by God. **Genesis 20:20-27. THE KING JAMES VERSION**

> [20]*Noah, a man of the soil, proceeded to plant a vineyard.*

> [21]*When he drank some of its wine, he became drunk and lay uncovered inside this tent.* [22]*Ham, the father of Canaan, saw his father naked and told his two brothers outside.* [23]*But Shem and Japheth took a*

garment and laid it across their shoulders; then they walked in backward and covered their father's nakedness. Their faces were turned the other way so that they would not see their father naked. [24]When Noah awoke from his wine and found out what his youngest son had done to him, [25]he said,

"Cursed be Canaan!

The lowest of Slaves

Will he be to his brothers."

[26]He also said,

Praise be to the Lord,

The God of Shem!

May Canaan be the slave of Shem.

[27]May God extend Japheth's

Territory; may Japheth's live

In the tents of Shem, and may

Canaan be the slave of Japheth".

For those who are not well versed in "Biblical Science", nor anthropology, it has been agreed upon by both religious scholars and anthropologist that there is only three race of people:

Negroid – Afrikans of Hamites

Mongoloid – Asians or Shemites

Caucasoid – Caucasians or Japhethies

Indoctrinations of subservient religious scriptures, images, and rituals by Caucasians ministers and Negro preachers were such as intoxicating ordeal that even in these days and time, Afrikan people are still drunken by the lies and deceit of wolves in sheep clothing. Religion has always been an effective method of controlling the thoughts and action of people. With distorted scriptures and falsified interpretations of Afrikan History, it was easy for slave-makers to annihilate the identity of Afrikan people and embed a totally new, but inferior name and self-worth into the psyche of this new being – **The Negro.**

Other Scriptures used by slave-makers:

DEUTERONOMY 7: 1 – 2

The Command to Conquer Canaan

[1] *"When the Lord your God brings you into the land which you go to possess, and has cast out many nations before you, the Hittites and the Girgashites and the Amorites and the Canaanites and the Perizzites and the Hivites and the Jebusites seven nations greater and mightier than you,*

[2] *and when the Lord your God delivers them over to you, you shall conquer them and utterly destroy them. You shall make no covenant with them nor show mercy to them.*

ISAIAH 20: 3 – 5

[3] *"Just as my servant Isaiah has walked naked and barefoot three years (300 years of slavery in America) for a sign and a wonder against Egypt and Ethiopia,* [4] *So shall*

the King of Assyria (Leuco – Syrian – White Syrian) lead away the Egyptians as prisoners and the Ethiopians as captives, young and old, naked and barefoot, with their buttocks uncovered, to the shame of Egypt. [5] *Then they (Black descendants) shall be afraid and ashamed of Ethiopia their expectation and Egypt their glory."*

Does this sound familiar?

Upon the abduction of Afrikans from their villages and nearby settlements. **Slave Trappers or Catchers** would bound trains of Afrikans (men, women, and children) with fetters and chains, strip them on their garments and tribal regalia; and march them to the Atlantic coastline to be board on slave ships.

Not only did this traumatic experience bring shame and disgrace, but the taken of their garments and regalia meant that they could no longer be identified by tribes, region or even as a nation of people.

One of the most repeated scripture by slave-makes and owners was:

EPHESIANS 6: 5 – 8

[5] *Slaves, obey your earthly masters with respect and fear, and with sincerity of heart, just as you would obey Christ.*

[6] *Obey them not only to win their favor when their eye is on you but as slaves of Christ, doing the will of God from your heart.*

[7] *Serve wholeheartedly as if you were serving the Lord, not people,*

[8] *because you know that the Lord will reward each one for whatever good they do, whether they are slave or fee.*

Scriptures such as these were given to Negro preachers by white slave-owning preachers, to preach to their congregation on Sundays. Black preachers were not allowed to preach in the same churches as white preachers, so slave congregated in barns, pastures, or where ever their owners permitted them to meet. Thus, Sunday became sore of a holiday (Holy Day) for slaves for the very fact that, they didn't have to work the fields if they stayed in church all day. Slave owners used these Negro preachers, not only as slaves but also as tools to keep the rest of the slaves blind to themselves, so that they could master them. Their goal was and still is to keep illiterate, which means ignorant.

9) Why does he fear the Devil now that he is a big man?

In Chancellor D. Williams book, *The Destruction of Black Civilization,* in the preview section subtitle – The European Journey; (pp 24), he gives a synopsis of the yoke that bounds Afrikan people to a psychological chain on Black inferiority.

> "I was already fully aware of the disastrous effect of the White American Education system on Black Americans who, not having any other frame of reference, had to adopt the ideologies and viewpoints of whites order to survive, even when those viewpoints were against them."

10) Because the Devil taught him to eat the wrong foods.

As the Institution of slavery progressed, the physical chains slowly loosened and the mental chains quickly tightened. For many Blacks in antebellum time sand post-Emancipation, accepting the status of "sub-hue-man beings" was a reality not only associated with slavery, but had become a field of study for Institutions of higher learnings. The fictitious stories of a "Black, primitive, savage race of peoples" had ceased being an oral folklore; and became the textbook history of the Afrikan people.

By means of preparatory schools and universities, the indoctrination of slavery (Black inferiority and White superiority) was propagate to a people who did not know their origin in this world. Therefore, years after the abolishment of chattel slavery, Afrikan people were still being ensnared into a web of mental slavery which expressed itself in an outward, cowardly manner.

11) Does that have anything to do with the above question #10?

In Lynch's closing speech, he spoke upon the "creation of a multiplicity of phenomenal of illusions" or in layman's term – A web of deception, a mental state of *deaf, dumb, and blindness*. As inscribed earlier in this text, the purpose, reason, and effects of Menticide caused an entire nation of Afrikan people to become betwixt by the occult system of the Anglo-Saxon. Questions #11 enquire about the statement in #10. So what question does #11 refers to? In following a lesson in the *Supreme Wisdom* booklet, entitled *Lost, Found Musilin*, lesson #2 or (1 – 40), the tenth question asked in this lesson is:

> *10. Who is that Mystery God?*

> Since antiquity, Afrikan people have always had an intimate relationship with a "Creator of all" and have practiced many different forms of spiritual-worshipping. In fact, it was Afrika that first taught the known world of the "Reality of God". However, it was believed by foreigners that the Gods of Afrikan were mystical, and because of this misconception, other cultures invented super-natural replicas (unseen, mystery Gods) and begin to worship that which they knew not of. The religious aspects of Christianity were taught to Europeans (Gentiles) by Afrikan prophets and teachers, Acts 13:1

> Barnabas, Simeon who was called Niger (N.W. Afrika) Lucious of Cyrene (N. Afrika)

for their earthly and divine salvation. Just as the laws and customs of Islam were given to mulatto Arabs by Black Arabians to bring them back into the fold of Afrikan moralities after they had perversely strayed after the "gods of Europe" and other countries.

Pantheism has always been practiced amongst Afrikan people. It's the ancient belief that – every living thing. This belief, once observed by European foreigners, was deemed as paganistic idol-worshipping; because their "materialistic" minds could not perceive the spiritual wisdom and knowledge of Afrikan people. So by their own selfish iniquities; they felt the need to force their religious beliefs upon a tranquil race of people whom they considered to be soul-less heathens.

The acceptance of this **"Mystery God"** was the turning point for Afrikan people. Not only was this subservient dogma untrue, but the Asiatic people that depended on this so-called mystery God for food, shelter, clothing, and freedom received nothing but slavery, hungriness, nakedness, and out of doors and was also beaten and killed by the ones who advocated that kind of God.

12) Negro n. (ne' gro) a member of a socially disadvantaged class of persons.

The etymology of this adjective… Negro is rooted in the dialect of ancient Europe, notably the Greeks and Romans. This word is a so-called derivative of the word Niger, pronounced /ni 'jer, nez-Her'/: and was used to describe a river in West Afrika that contained "Black" water and the people that inhabited that land. Before the arrival of Caucasian foreigners, the term Niger or Negro was never used to describe a native tribe base on the complexion of their skin, nor in a general aspect of the color black. Upon the conquest and colonization of Afrikans by these northern invaders, the names Niger, Negro – from which derived Negrito and Ethiopian was placed upon the original people, which caused a separate division besides tribalism. From this intervention came **Classism** or for a better terminology; a social caste system which was based solely on lighter-skin versus darker-skin. It was during this era in time that the status-quo of the entire known world was reversed, and the **Par excellence of "Beautiful Blackness of Skin"**, became the scorn of the earth.

Black, according to science means death, wicked, evil, dark; nothing good, i.e., Black-out… (Unconscious). With these meanings in mind, Negro (Black) in the Latin language could be an alternative form of **Necro,** which also means death, dead body, those that are dead; one that is dead (unconscious). Considering that Europeans believed that the people they had encountered were soulless heathens, and deemed their rituals and ceremonies honoring their dead, paganistic taboo. We can assert that the descriptive term neco was used to indicate a people considered as "A dead (unconscious) race of "Human Beings", and thus the idiom – "THE DARK CONTINENT" was placed on Afrika. It was this racist assumption that opened the door for a white supremacist conquest and gave birth to the Afikan slave trade.

E: The Phenomenon Substantial Original Historical Base

A man's history bears witness to his identity and his existence. The Trans-Atlantic Slave Trade, along with the William Lynch slave making system, has separated the consciousness; of the 17+ millions of Afrikans here in the wilderness of North America. A closer examination of history would reveal that it was through these two systems, that European enslavers were able to obliterate the identity of their Afrikan possessions. Within the conscious lies, an awakeness, an external and internal awareness; and the identity of a person. Without these three principles, a person is said to be brain dead; mentally unconscious and physically lamed, thus a Negro.

Identity involves the ideas of them and space. No two identities can dwell in the same space at the same time which means that a Negro cannot be physically free if he is unaware of his mental and spiritual enslavement.t As long as a person thinks that he or she is a Negro, they will remain a slave of a mental death and power.

There have never been any species on the Earth-land that has had more identities than the American Negro. He has been everything besides himself; such as coon, buck, spade, shine; speck, sam-bo, sideshow, pimp, hustler, gangster, thug, hoodlum, beast, gorilla, dog; and the grandest of them all –**A READ NIGGER.** Being that a Negro has no definite identity because "it" has no self-worth, it cannot be identified with the known nations of the world. There is no such place as Negro-Land, nor is a

Negro an actual human being; it only acts as a personification of an Afrikan.

However, for the Negro, there is a possibility of a resurrection because the lost and found were once "mentally" dead and many of them revived from it because they were not physically dead, only mentally dead. Knowing that the Negro is a **Strawman,** a person who has lost the knowledge of himself and is living a beast life, who is also easily led in the wrong direction and hard to lead in the right direction. To civilize him and teach him how to be himself and accept his own, along with the science of everything life; *Love, Peace, and Happiness.* These questions must be answered before the healing process can begin and the Negro is no longer *deaf, dumb, and blinded* to the reality of his slave masters.

1. What is the Negro problem?

Answer: The Negro problem is a state of mental inconstancy. Because the Negro was made, and made mentally weak and dependent, his spiritual, moral, and psychological faculties are wavery unto the point of instability. What a Negro is today, he may not be tomorrow. It is this that makes the Negro untrustworthy, manipulative, obscurant, and Judas to his people and the cause of uplifting falling humanity.

2. How can the Negro escape the "multiplicity" of phenomena of illusions?

Answer: First, the Negro must recognize and admit that "He doesn't know, what he doesn't know", (deaf, dumb, and blind). The Negro knows that he is under-educated, underemployed, and under-housed, but they do not try to find out who it is that causes all these things to happen by letting the *poor righteous teachers* teach them. They rather believe in the "rich slave makers" of the poor on face value that the reason things are the way they are is because they don't possess the intelligence to improve their conditions. Secondly, the Negro must know that he is not a Negro, colored, Afrikan-American, convict; prisoner or inmate because it is through these names that the slave makers are able to identify their property. These names may not mean mothering to the Negro, however, they symbolize a spiritual, mental and national death.

3. What is his own self?

Answer: [1] His own self is a righteous Asiatic Black Man. Righteous, meaning one having Knowledge, Wisdom, Understanding culture and power/refinement, and is not a salvage in a pursuit of happiness. Asiatic and Afrikan is synonymous, Asiatic means aboriginal of the planet Earth. [2] Those under the Asiatic Covenant. Black means Supreme Intelligent, Divinity, Infinite Wisdom. [3] Black, n. Melanin. Man means, the Supreme being, the Highest in existence. Man himself is not the body, nor soul, he is a spirit and a thought of the Almighty Infinite God, therefore man, the original man has no beginning or end.

Once the Negro recognize that the True and Living God is the Son of Man, the Supreme being a Black man from Asia, who teaches Freedom, Justice, and Equality to all the Human Family of the Planet Earth; that his Heaven and Hell is not above nor beneath, but the conditions of his mind which he; himself creates. Once he knows the truth and disavow the falsified (mis)-education and (mist)-emancipation of this enslavers, and fully accept his rightful position among the affairs of men and the nations of the world, then and only then will be become what his ancient forefathers were, without doubt, or contradiction.

4. Can the Negro be re-born back into his own culture, that of the Asiatic Nations of the Planet Earth?

Answer: Before I answer this question, I want to first establish a clear and concise definition of "culture", as used in this text. An in-depth study of history will prove that the original people: The Asiatic Black Family of the planet Earth has always defined themselves as a GOD CENTERED CULTURE. Our natural ways of life are centered around" And Universal GOD, Nature, and the Universal laws governing all events according to all Holy and Divine scriptures, i.e., The Holy Qur'an and Bible, which is the history of the original man.

The first man was created from sounding black mud. (ALMUNTADA ALISMAIC version, Su'rah 15:b) or of dust of the ground (King James version, Genesis 2:7). This not only makes a man a part of nature, but also the Maker, the Owner, and the Cream of the planet Earth. I also stated that God breathed into his (man) nostrils the breath of life (Bible). In the Qur'an in Surah 15 verse 29, it states: "And when I have proportioned him and breathed into him on my (Created) soul, (the elements of life)."

This is why the original people are so spiritual and refer to ourselves as "Soul Brothers and Soul Sisters". It further states that the original man was given dominion over the earth and was taught the laws concerning agriculture, mating, karma, righteous knowledge, and tricknowledge: Love, Truth, Freedom, Justice, and Equality. It was these laws that formatted the first Holy and Divine Creed and established and a covenant with the great Universal God. This is the original man, woman, and child culture – Peace and the submission to their *higher* self.

So to answer the above question… **Can the Negro be reborn back into their culture?** It is taught to us that only some of the American Negroes revived from the mental death of slaver. It is fact, that a person doesn't change their condition until they are 1000% dissatisfied with their current state of mind and body. Because the Negro is a product with no comprehensible identity, they are satisfied being classed as uncivilized people, poisoned animal eaters, slaves of mental death and power…sheep of the worst kind, with a world for a shepherd.

To be reborn means to humble ourselves as babes, then unshackle and unchain our minds from the psychological bondage of slavery and Jim Crowism, and be willing to be re-educated, rebirth, and re-accepted back into the Human Family.

Out of the 85% of the American Negro who has lost the knowledge of themselves, their GOD, and their native land and is living a savage way of life, only some of them will return back into their rightful self. In order to be recognized as a citizen and part and parcel of a specific government, one must duly proclaim his or her rightful Nationality, Birth-Right, and Native Creed.

In a quote by Noble Drew Ali, he states:

> Nationality is the foundation of mankind and whosever fails to proclaim his nationality is a slave in whosoever land he finds himself in."

The **Naturalization Law of 1790**, only allowed **Free White Person"** to claim citizenship. In 1857, the Supreme Court ruled that a person of African descent could not become a citizen. Although the 14th Amendment gives citizenship to "All persons born or naturalized in the United States", the "Freedman Law" states: *The status of a newborn child depends on the status of the mother. If she was free, the child was free, if she was a slave, the child was a slave, thus slavery is inheritable."*

This brings us to the point of examining the term, "African America". According to Scott, Foresman Intermediate Dictionary (concerning) **African-American or (Afro-American), of American Negroes.**

2. An American Negro

For those who prefer to call themselves African American is just a fancy way of saying - I'm an American Slave". It's another illusional identity that white racist dictators gave feeble-minded Negroes to keep them from complaining about words such as Colour Folks, Black people, Negroes, and Niggers.

Just because they put African in front of the word American, that separates the "Master and slave relationship". By stating it like that, an American (slave Master) identifying ourselves as Afrikan-American does not give us the liberation of independence we need to re-establish ourselves as a separate and equal nation on American soil or to –relink ourselves back to a specified nation or native land. Clinging on to anything that links us to slavery, like sharecropping of tenure farming. When the U.S. so-called abolished slavery, some slaves stayed on the plantations slaving in fields and made their 'Massa" rich off their labor.

Knowledge about our-history and our-self, the more independent we become about our-history and our-self, the more independent we become as a Nation. We, as "New Afrikans" cannot and will not save all our brothers and sisters who have accepted being slaves and still honor the term, "Negro".

In my conclusion of this chapter, for those who are dissatisfied being enslaved by a system that has oppressed, depressed, and repressed Afrikan people since the 1500's.

My solution to breaking free from the psychological and physical Peculiar Institution, escaping the web of the slave-making system is simply this…

ACCEPT YOUR OWN AND BE YOUR SELF

Love thy brotha, as thy love Self?

II

Death of Africanism:

The Willie Lynch 'system Re-Vised

A: Give Me Liberty, or Give Me Death

I know not what course others may take, but as for me,
give me liberty, or give me death!

Patrick Henry
March 1775

The history of America, as told by the textbooks, is a great tale of exploration; hardship, triumph, thanksgiving, bravery, and independents. Whereas, our history concerning America, is a tragic story of kidnapping, torture; murder, rape, austerity, slavery and every other kind of malicious treatment and atrociousness unrecorded by HIS-STORY books.

Despite the failed attempts of Caucasian slave makers to decimate 'Afrikan Consciousness and Consciences', great cultural and intellectual minds till ascended out of the ghastly system of slavery. Little by little, Afrikan customs and beliefs slowly re-entered back into the daily lives of the four million plus slaves in the wilderness of North American. Afrikan folklores and ancestral stories were introduced to the slaves by newly arriving Afrikans who still held glimpses of memories of their once native home.

"More than three hundred and fifty years ago, Afrikans were first brought to this country to be sold into slavery. Forbidden formal education, slaves served at the pleasure of their white masters and learned only the anguish of unrewarded toil. The "Self-Evident" truth contained within the Declaration of Independence that all persons are created equal had no application to the slave. The slave was neither free nor equal. Commenting on whether the framers of the Constitution considered slaves to be included within the phrase "We the People", Chief Justice (Roger B.) Taney penned the following remarks in the Dred Scott case:

We think they are not... (and) were not intended to be included... They had for more than a century before been regarded as beings of an inferior order, and altogether unfit to associate with the white race...and so far inferior, that the Negro of the Afrikan race was regarded as an article of property, and held, and bought and sold as such...

> Scott v. Sanford. 60 U.S.
> (19 How.) 393,405,407-18,15 L. Ed. 691 (1857)

What you just read is the opinion of Judge Harold Murphy; in the Civil Action of:

> "John F. Knight, Jr. et al., vs. The State of Alabama, et al., Civil Action No. CV-83-M-1676-S (Northern District of Ala., July 11, 1983)"

To fully comprehend the deep-seeded racist conviction of the AmeriKKKan fabric, we must first know and understand exactly what racism really is and the two types of racism, with its three hideous forms;

> Racism [rey-siz-uh m] noun

1. a belief or doctrine that inherent differences among the various human racial groups determine cultural or individual achievement, usually involving the idea that one's own race is superior and has the right to dominate others or that a particular racial group is inferior to the others.
2. a policy, system of government, etc., based upon or fostering such a doctrine; discrimination.
3. hatred or intolerance of another race or other races.[iii]

Genetic racism [jƏnet´ik/adj., / rey-siz-uh m/n.]

1. Hereditary repulsion
2. The aversion between two naturally opposing bodies.
3. Natural enmity.

Adopted racism   [uh-dopt]/adj., / rey-siz-uh m/n/]

1. Awareness and acceptance of social divisions and one's place in them.
2. Espouse.

The three forms of racism are:

Overt racism

1. Acts done or demonstrated openly.
2. Unconcealed, not hidden.

An example of overt racism is the: Vertical violence perpetrated directly by the colonial states coercive institutions. I.e., hate groups, police, schools, courts, prisons, etc...

Invert racism

1. To reverse the position, order, or relation of.

Invert racism is displayed in the nature of horizontal violence, the response to a colonial relationship used to impose violence on an oppressed group of people by containing them in a constant state of poverty and repression, so that they lash out against each other, thus forwarding the agenda of the oppressor.

Convert racism

1. Is hidden, secret or disguised racist feelings, intents, or motives.

"If you want to hide something from a Black person, put it in a Book!"

For years we have heard this saying, we told it as a joke, we laughed at it as a joke; even when it was not meant to be a joke, we still didn't take it seriously.

Usually, secrecy is from evil ends, or from questionable motives, or because the person seeking secrecy is ashamed of himself and knows that if his act of motives become known, he would make himself odious, and his ulterior motives obvious.

B: A New Oppression

The history, politics, and policies of all southern states, but those of Alabama in particular, must take into consideration the essential thread of racism and the matricidal effects of its Peculiar Institution. The Law of White Supremacy and Black Inferiority found daily expression and constant application throughout the years of Post-Emancipation.

The wars freed more than 4 million Afrikans from chattel slavery, but their social, political, economical and educational positions in the former slaveholding states were still undefined. The following era called Reconstruction is one of the most paradoxical times ever recorded by Historian. President Lincoln hoped for reconstruction was that it would "bind up the nation's wounds", caused by the Civil War. However, it was during the era of reconstruction of the REBELLIOUS Confederate, the topic of the political forum, and once again the subject matter of:

"Should [They] or should they not be counted for purposes of representation?"

It was this question that caused a hysterical uproar in 1787 when southerners wanted slaves counted towards representation in the U.S. House of Representatives, while still insisting that [They] were property. Northerners protested they debated that since Negroes could not vote, they should not be counted. The end results of this debate came to be known as THE 3/5 (three-fifths) of a person", which means that three out of every five people of Afrikan origin, equals one person of the European race. Also included was the emission by Congress to let slavery continue for at least 20 years.

With a presumption of freedom, Afrikans quickly turned towards politicians to improve their conditions. Because the Republicans contested against the southern slaveholding states, and campaigned for the abolition of slavery, Freedmen, as they were called, clinched on to the (Radical) Republican bandwagon. Those Republicans that came south during this era were called Carpetbagger: merely because they traveled with a popular form of luggage of that time made from carpet material.

White southerners viewed such persons as unscrupulous, dishonest profit-seekers who came south to loot and plunder and had for the most part; they

Interfered, in a negative way, with the master and slave relationship; and violated their legal rights to own slaves.

White southerners who had cast their lot with these Radicals and Freedmen were called Scalawags. Scalawags were more hated by white southerners than Carpetbaggers because whites felt that they were traitors against their own race and considered them to be the "scorn of the Confederacy".

The southern opponents to the Radical Republicans et al…were referred to as conservatives, though the name Democrats or by a more common term, Dixiecrats were a sufficiently accurate title. Nothing made these white southerners more bitter and resentful than to be "ruled by the very people they had totally dominated for years", in spite of the fact that the majority of their so-called Black Republican Government (now known as the Black Caucus) were white carpetbaggers and scalawags. Although there were a few Caucasian white people that were sincere I the tooth and nail fight for equal rights for Afrikans, the course sentiments (of the Radical Republications) is best expressed in the words of their most honored Republican President; Abraham Lincoln:

"On the point of my wanting to make war between the free and the slave states, there has been no issue between us. So, too, when he (Douglas) assumes that I am in favor of introducing a perfect social and political equality between the black and white races. There are false issues…

Lincoln and Douglas Debate
Alton, Ill. Oct. 15, 1858

For political gain and Plutocratic power, overt racism masked itself behind handshakes' smiles, parental achievements; and the subliminal wording of the two additional amendments to the U.S. Constitutions.

Most historians view the reconstruction years as a 'Tragic era', stating that Lincoln's expectations and his resolution of "malice toward none" was a sure failure. However, historian and activist W.E.B DuBois stated in his documentary entitled Black Reconstruction that: Reconstruction was an effort by both whites and blacks to create a truly democratic society, it failed because it did not go far enough; one fact and one alone explains the attitude of whites toward reconstruction, they cannot conceive of Negroes as men.

Kenneth Stampp wrote in *The Era Of Reconstruction* (1965), that: the Radicals were genuine reformers out to defend the rights of blacks and that most black legislators had been good public servants. Moreover, they had never dominated the state governments of the period. Reconstruction failed not because of what it did to whites in the south, but because it did not implement the reforms necessary to ensure African Americans equal rights.

Amendment XII

Section 1. Neither slavery nor involuntary servitude, except as a punishment for crime whereof the party shall have been duly convicted, shall exist within the United States, or any place subject to their jurisdiction.

By the end of 1865, all the southern state governments had ratified the new 13 Amendment to the constitution. After the abolishment of chattel slavery, frivolous laws called Black Codes were enacted to keep blacks in a condition of semi-slavery and to ensure that they did not receive the equal protection of the laws. These subordinated policies and laws were designed to institutionalize segregation, and solidly a Confederate Colonial Domination while assuring the inferior status of Afrikan progression.

The 13th Amendment has within its context what is called an Exception Clause. Since we are dealing with the philosophy of law, to comprehend what is meant by except in the 13th Amendment; we must consult the BLACK'S LAW DICTIONARY for a clear understanding.

ex·cept   1: To take or leave out

ex·cep·tion: 1: Something that is excepted or excluded.
                 2: The retention of an existing right or
                    interest; esp: exclusion of a section of
                    real property from a conveyance.

Clause, n.   1: A distinct section or provision of a legal
                    document or instrument.

Justice Oliver Wendell Homes in: Towne Vs. Eisner, 245 U.S. 418,425 (1918) held that: Oliver Wendell Holmes Jr. wrote, "a word is not a crystal, transparent and unchanged; it is the skin of a living thought and may vary greatly in color and content according to the circumstances and time in which it is used." THE CONSTITUTION![iv]

The Constitution is the Forked Tongue of the Serpent of Eden. It's the tree of good and evil, in which no unconscious man can digest its fruit. On the face of it, it is just, but beneath its racist surface- it is Just-ICE. There are two basic ways to interpret the U.S. Constitution. They are the Frozen and Evolutionary Theories.

The Frozen Theory is basically interpreting the U.S. Constitution in the same way as the creators did during their own time. There are three (3) sources drawn from to accomplish this:

1. Convention Notes of 1787;
2. Letters written between delegates of the time;
3. Literature (books) written during this time.

The Evolutionary Theory is quite the opposite. It represents the basic attitudes of society as it develops. The interpretation of the U.S. Constitution through the evolutionary theory can be seen in many ways.

We, as Afrikan people must not consider it to be a coincidence, that after the ratification of the 13th Amendment; that the former slaveholding states enacted laws and policies to revert its "use to be property' back into a subservient state of being. There laws and policies, which President Andrew Johnson upheld, is the 'exception clause' mention previously and is a result of a "Behind the Lodge Door" convention between Union policymakers and Confederate law enforcers. The three sources of the frozen theory are what is excluded from the 13th Amendment.

The economic power of the south depended on slave labor. To take away the very thing that provided financial stability to the southern states without replacing it with a system better or equal to the manual labor furnished by slaves, would have meant a collapse of the entire monetary network of the United States as a whole.

C: Black Codes

Reconstruction came to an end in all of the former slaveholding states as a result of "the Corrupt Bargain" of

1877. Some may say it was a political compromise to resolve the disputed 1876 Presidential elections between Rutherford B. Hayes and Samuel J. Tilden, in which Hayes became the 19th President of the United States of America. Hayes agreed to pull all federal troops from those southern states still occupied by its military and to end "provisional governments" and marital law. He also promised to appoint a conservative southerner to his cabinet.

Alabama reconstruction had officially ended in November of 1874, when the "Conservative Democratic Party" swept all state offices, elected former confederates to both chambers of the state legislature, and reclaimed most of the county government offices across the state. After 1877, the white citizens of the north turned their backs on the blacks in the south, leaving them to fend for themselves in a time of overt repression. Immediately, the white Conservative Democrats broke their promise to guarantee blacks their own rights and t let them vote. Step by step whites deprived blacks of common and civil rights and reluctantly reduced them to 2nd class citizens.

Although the Civil Rights Act of 1875 provided specifically that "Citizens of every race and color" were entitled to "the full and equal enjoyments of all public places", the Redeemers and the whites in the south began to gore laws set forth by the radicals of the north. In the "New South" whites governed blacks by a different set of laws, laws which only benefited whites and preserved their "Confederate Citizens" ways of life. The new party stood for white supremacy, low taxes, few government services and segregation of the races. Many state officials were former Confederates, all 18th-century governors of Alabama after the 1878 Constitution enacted the notorious "Black Codes" for the ordinance and maintenance of black inferiority.

Black Codes: were state laws governing the activity and status of Negroes in the south after the civil war. When slavery was abolished in 1805, southerners used Black Codes which was upheld and agreed upon by President Andrew Johnson to retain control over the freedmen.

The Black Codes reflected the views of the previous Slave Codes. Alabama adopted these laws upon its admission to the Union in 1819. Black Codes varied in strictness and in detail from state to state. These laws and policies put restraints on the liberties of blacks living in the south. Some laws forbade Negroes to testify in court unless he was a witness of the party in a legal action. Negroes could not carry firearms, meet in unsupervised groups, or seduce other Negroes for the purpose of malicious intent.

In certain states, Negroes could not own land nor purchase tangible property without giving proof of where they got the money from. They were also made liable to criminal prosecution rather than civil punishment for breaking labor contracts.

In Alabama, the Legislature, like those in most southern states, enacted a stature, making it a crime to instruct any Negro, young or old; free or slave, in the arts of reading and writing. Punishment for such crimes ranged from lashes on the bare back to being reverted back into servitude by conviction; to being hung by the neck, for "freedmen" who refused to adhere to fictitious labor contracts. They were illegally arrested and railroad by the courts, then sentence to Work Houses, whereupon the person upholding the contract would pay off the judge and acquire his (the Freedmen) service for the duration of this sentence.

After the Conservative Democrats took office, the first issue they addressed was the voting rights of black people living in the south. They wanted to change the state's constitution to deny voting privileged to blacks. Their plan was to set up barriers to make it difficult or virtually impossible for black people to vote. Some of the by-laws included within the Black Codes were:

Poll Taxes: a required fee a voter must pay each time they vote;

Literacy tests: were made-up exams, which required blacks to read a section of the constitution or some other document and explain what they just read, or they were told to read a certain word and then asked the word's meaning.

Alabama Constitution of 1901, Art. VIII, § 177 gave the right to vote to all males, but they had to be at least twenty-one years-old of age, of good character and free of guilt of any one of more than thirty crimes. These crimes included: reckless eyeballing, spitting on the sidewalk, and disorderly conduct towards white people; treason, murder, arson, perjury; embezzlement, assault, burglary, robbery, forgery, wife beating, bigamy; vagrancy and various sex crimes.

Good Character Clause; allowed voting registration to registrant citizens who were disqualified for other reasons as long as they understood their duties as a citizen and had residence requirements of two years in the state, six months in the county and three months in the precinct.

Grandfather Clause; allowed ex-veterans or descendants of veterans who had served honorably in any United States war. This clause helped many white males get around other restrictions.

Vagrancy Act: All free Negroes and Mulattoes over the age of eighteen must have written proof of a job at the beginning of every year.

Because of the passing of the Civil Rights Acts, we really don't think of the word Disfranchise.

Disfranchise means to deprive of the right to vote. We believe in these modern day and time that the laws and policies of Antebellum south, post-emancipation and the Civil Rights era do not apply to us. We should never forget that during slavery, as diabolical as those times were; white supremacy was just a small serpent in the garden, whispering suggestions. But as time passed and as it went to and from across the earth seeking the devour, all the HE can, and they grew. Now in its full stage of development, IT, HE, THEY have become a monstrous Dragon waging war against the GODLY people, and just as HE promised.

Its tail shall take out a third of the Lost-found Asiatic people of North American and all over the world.

D: The Wrath of Jim Crow

Alabama is a state in which its contenders have always worn the badge of white supremacy on their sleeve and has been since its founding, a state that is overtly boastfully and unapologetic for its racist conviction.

In the Heart of Dixie, Anglo-Saxon colonialism is a "thing" almost guaranteed and confided as subconscious rules and "ways of life."

During the times when Jim Crowism was practiced overtly, Black people were treated as "beings of an inferior order", therefore, their private and public lives were burdened by the constant antagonism of these laws and policies.[v]

*The first Migration-1890s

- Jim Crow began 1890 with the separate but equal justification that permitted racial segregation
- It was a code of conduct that regulated African Americans to 2nd class citizenship
- The origins of Jim Crow has been attributed to "Jump Jim Crow", a song-and-dance caricature of blacks performance by white actor Thomas D. Rice in black face.

Jim Crow

- The Great Migration(1890s)-People were moving out of the South to the North in large numbers
  - Mobility is an important part of freedom. People were travelling to get "the boot" off their necks. Blacks moving from the South created a problem for the agrarian south, it was about agency and identity

The first Migration-1890s

Black men were rendered powerless, not because they did not possess the abilities to substantiate their manhood, but because they consumed a fallacy which internalized fear. If a white man was to decide that he wanted to have sex with a black man's wife, he would simply tell the husband to wait outside on the porch until he's finished having his way with his wife. The fear of death would often sway the husband to obey his command.

The Jim Crow was the renascence of the Black Codes. Jim Crow laws were state laws and district ordinances enacted from the end of Radical Reconstruction, through the first seven deceased of the twentieth century for the purpose of mandating de jure (in accordance with law) racial segregation. It is noted that the reality of Jim Crow comes from a popular minstrel show.

Thomas "Daddy" Rice, who wrote a song and dance called "Jim Crow" in 1832, was a white man who painted his face black with burnt cork soot, dressed in rags and sang and danced in a caricature of blacks. This disparaging portrayal was of a crippled slave named 'Jim', who belonged to a white man named 'Crow'. The joyful grinning and 'buck dancing' was the part of his show he called 'Jump Jim Crow. This public ridiculing amused his white audience, and the term quickly became a household name.

Separation seemed less important when black people were in slavery and was considered as personal property. In the south, the segregation of the races was as common as the morning sun. Tennessee passed the first Jim Crow law in 1881, followed by Florida in 1887, Texas in 1889, and then Alabama and Mississippi. Most justices of that time had ruled that the Civil Rights Act of 1875 was unconstitutional, and therefore it was not illegal for an owner of a private business to practice racial segregation. Although the Fourteenth Amendment clearly stated:

> Section 1: All person born or naturalized in the United States, and subject to the jurisdiction thereof, are citizens of the United States and of the state wherein they reside. No state shall make or enforce any law which shall abridge the privileges or immunities of citizens of the United States; nor shall any state deprive any person of life, liberty, or property, without due process of law; nor deny to any person within its jurisdiction the equal protection of the laws.

Most Supreme Court Justices interpreted it as "protections against actions by the state government, not by private person. Some may say that the separation of the races "de jure", was unjust and unconstitutional. However, it was doing these times of racial segregation that Black-Economics was at its apex. Black people spent their money on black-owned businesses, bought products made by black companies, and built up black communities with black money. In 1896, the Supreme Court ruled in the civil case of:

> Plessy vs. Ferguson, 163 U.S. 537 (1896), established the legality of racial segregation so long as facilities were kept "separate but equal".

Many have debated about the effects the "separate but equal" law had on black people as a whole. Some assert that since Afrikan people residing in America were deemed legally free and independent; that the best solution should have been establishing their own socio-political and economical system within this system. Others refute this by stating that, separate but equal really meant that Black people would get "equal quantity", but not "equal quality", so to guarantee both, Blacks needed to integrate with White people. After integration, Blacks became eagerly to spend their money with White own businesses.

At once, Mr. Charlie "ice" was colder than Black people "ice". This psychosis is still prominent in Black communities today. Studies have shown that a single legal tender (a one dollar bill) only circulates within the Black community twenty-four (24 hours before it's in the pockets of white business owners.

Despite the many accomplishment Blacks have achieved since the Supreme overturned the Plessy decision with the:

> Brown vs. Board of Education of Topeka, 347 U.S. 483 (1954): 349 U.S. 294 (1955), ruling, many still believe that Black American would have achieved greater, without the many influences of White people. And although integration is the law, separation is still the reality. Blacks are still sectioned off in lower-class districts, and Whites are still segregated in their secluded suburban neighborhoods. Pre-eminent Black schools are well underfunded and ill-equip with second-handed learning material that's years behind majority White schools. The limited rights and privileges that integration did produce in Black communities are often overshadowed by introverted

racism and the cognition of Puppetry of Black politician.

Ever since the abolishment of chattel slavery, the political and social status of Asiatic Black people has been the impetus which has urged Europeans to constantly and effectively create arbitrary systems designed to legalize inferiority of Black people. On the point of the Supreme Law of America, it is written"

For Satan (Racism) himself is transformed into an angel of light (Truth). Therefore it is no great thing if his ministers also be transformed as the ministers of righteousness. (2nd Corinthians, 11:14)

The word constitution, according to Merriam Webster's Dictionary of Law (1828); means Constitution n. (Latin constitution system, fundamental principles of an institution), form constituter to set up, establish 1: the basic principles and laws of a nation, state, or social group that determine the powers and duties of the government and guarantee certain rights to the people in it 2: a written instrument containing the fundamental rules of a political or social organization.

When the U.S. adopted the 13th, 14th, and 15th Amendment, to a dogma that beforehand excluded Black people from its social equality, it presented a pretense that this is the "Land of the free and the home of the brave". Given the circumstances that Black people were ascending from one of the triple stages of enslavement, and in many forms still barred from the enjoyment of fundamental education. The bias comprehension of its words evaded the awareness of its subjects. The 14th amendment guaranteed equal protection of the law, but it did make racial separation, or separation illegal. It did not even tell southern states to permit Black people to vote.

"When Blacks ceased to have an influence on elections, elected officials stop paying attention to their needs and wants." ~ Frederick Douglas.

Alabama was granted statehood on December 14, 1819, months before that on July 5, forty-four delegates met in Huntsville to prepare a constitution for some to be the STATE OF ALABAMA. The Constitution of 1819 was modified twice, during and after the Civil War.

The 1861 Constitution was passed when Alabama became part and parcel of the Confederate States of America.

After that came the Constitution of 1865, which was drawn up after the defeat of the Confederacy and the end of the Civil War. This paradoxical document outlawed slavery in the southern states. Next came the Constitution of 1868, under Radical Republicans, which gave voting rights to black and white males. In the same year, the fourteenth amendment of the U.S. Constitution was passed, declaring all person "born or naturalized in the United States to be citizens".

When the white south was told to regard Blacks as 'Human Beings', and to respect them as citizens, they immediately sought a new system to renounce their status as equals to whites. They knew that the current system of intimidation, acts, and threats of violence, fraudulent and illicit voting methods, and out-right murder when needed would soon cause the intervention of the federal government and the despicable Republican northerners.

In 1874, the conservative Democrats won all the statewide offices and both houses of the legislature. With this victory, the south proclaimed that it had "Redeem"…white rulership, eradicated Radical influence and that they had "put the Negroes back in their places".

The delegates quickly insisted that a constitutional convention be assembled to draw up what would be known as the 'Redeemer's Constitution of 1875'. This constitution would direct two objectives, (1) excommunicate Blacks form all-white Democratic incumbency, 2) forbid attendance of Black and White students in the same schools.

To guarantee Conservative Democratic sovereignty, the party (Klan) aim to manipulate or altogether eliminate the Black vote. During the actual convention, the delegates agreed to exclude a verbatim report of the proceedings. By doing so, it deprived the U.S. government of any evidence that could be used against them, and accuse the intervention of federal officials. Delegates to separate state elections from federal elections, and, thus, avoiding any interference from federal officers at voting sites.

On November 16, 1875; the Redeemer's Constitution was officially ratified and relentlessly reduce Blacks to second-class citizens. The first section: 'Equality and rights of men', was changed from "all men are created equal' to "That all men are equally free and independent:"

Skillful, the framers of the 1875 Constitution attacked Black educational and political gateways from all angles. Emmet O'Neal, a delegate of the 1875 and 1901 Constitutional Conventions and Governor of Alabama in 1910, spoke in front of the Alabama State Bar Association and said:

> White supremacy was maintained by methods which could only find their justification in the imperious necessity of ***self-defense and self-protection***. Negro rule meant that the white man must surrender his home and lands or remain under conditions which were intolerable. The white race had to settle Alabama and owned its lands and hence was determined not to surrender to a line and inferior race, which had been brought to Alabama as slaves and which had acquired the right to suffrage only by grants from the victories North, and as one of the results of the war.

One of the first attacks on black educational opportunities was the disbandment of the State Board of Education in Alabama.

*The constitutional convention of 1901

The (SBS) State Board of Education in Alabama was empowered to make laws and enforce laws which then had to be signed by the governor, or vetoed, with 3R's (Reading, Writing and Arithmetic) but far below the grade level of white student; and the second effect which I call the 4th R-Racial inferiority acceptance. How or better yet, why did we expect a people that have enslaved us... murdered us... RAPED us... and tarred and feather us...etc...etc...etc... to all of a sudden educate us?

E: Inferiority Complex and The Constitution of 1901

1) Inferiority complex n.: an acute sense of personal inferiority often resulting either in timidity or through overcompensation in exaggerated aggressiveness.

2: a collective sense of cultural, regional, or national inferiority.[vi]

I can still remember the pictures in my middle school American History books and those in my high school World Geography books. The photos of happy slaves picking cotton in big fields and half-naked Afrikans marching in trains with fetters around their necks and ankles. The history of 4,400,000 Afrikan people worldwide was always compiled in just 5 to 6 pages starting with so-called white Egyptians and ending with the normal selected Blacks. The facts were never taught to us that those same half-naked and happy Afrikans we read about were in the first inhabitants of the planet Earth and the first people to build a civilization. However, because we are educated in a white neo-colonized society, we learn more about the accomplishments of non-myelinated races, and we have spoofed Europeanized versions of African and Afrikans.

I remember not one of my peers wanted to be associated with Afrikan people mainly because of the shameful and degrading images they saw. We always made derogatory jokes about someone being an 'Afrikan Booty scratcher' or that their hair was 'nappier than an Afrikan with a headache'.

In the 80s, a lot of us became positively aware of our deep Afrikan roots by and through the influence of conscious rap music and rap artists.

Q. Why does the devil teach and keep our people so illiterate?

A. So that he can use them as a tool and also as a slave. He keeps them blind to themselves so that he can master them. Illiterate means ignorant.

After Reconstruction failed, it became open season on AmeriKKKa's' freed Afrikan population. It was reported that in one county in Alabama alone, they were averaging five lynching per week, an estimate of twenty Afrikans killed every month; that's about two-hundred-forty lynching in a years' time. Numerous schools, churches and other places where Blacks gathered to learn the basic educational skills were bombed and set afire. Whites knew that if Black Alabamians learned to read and write, they would eventually be urges to vote.

In 1891, Alabama passed the Apportionment Act which became a lawful way to allocate money levied from local and state taxes and divert a majority of it to fund all-white schools. The SBE was dominated by white supremacists and its members was charged with the obligation of distributing funds "just and equally". In the white south, this meant apportioning a substantial amount of the education of their children.

If you are reading this book, just stop and think about the school you attended. Just think about how inadequately funded your school was and probably still is. Now compare that to predominantly white schools.

Public school collects tax revenues from local businesses and other state taxes to equip its students with the best opportunities possible. However, most predominantly black schools are not located near the major business. And just like in 1891, a large portion of Alabama's' white conservative citizens today, still believe that their tax monies should go towards the funding of white schools and black parents should pay for their children's education.

There really was no way of securing funds "legally" to divert it towards white schools. The SBE was given a Carte Blanche which was a blank check endorsed by the state official, and a lump sum to divide per capita (equally to each) school. Since its members felt that white students would benefit the most from the money, they perverted more towards all-white schools. In schools where white students made up less than 20%, those schools received just enough to function. This dis-apportionment became a major problem for the SBE when white and black parents filed complaints against the board, claiming that there wasn't adequate funding for schools in rural areas. No one wanted to integrate the entire school system, nor did they want to provide black schools with equal funding.

One of the few solutions to this problem was to rid its current constitution of all tax restrictions, segregate/separate city and county schools, then distribute the funds to all white schools. To accomplish this, Alabama needed a new constitution, one that will reflect the views and opinion of white supremacists. A constitution that would not only accomplish this goal but would also extend the margin between "Black opportunities" and "White progress" and at the same time, disenfranchise Alabama's' Black population.

ALABAMAS' CONSTITUTION 1901

Revelation 6:8 King James Version (KJV)

[8]And I looked, and behold a pale horse: and his name that sat on him was Death, and Hell followed with him. And power was given unto them over the fourth part of the earth, to kill with sword, and with hunger, and with death, and with the beasts of the earth.[vii]

Pale- noun \ 'pāl \:

1. (of a person or a person's skin) light-colored or lacking in color: a pale complexion;
2. lacking the usual intensity of color due to fear, illness, stress, etc.:

3. of a low degree of chroma, saturation, or purity; approaching white or gray:
4. not bright or brilliant; dim:[viii]

Death- noun \ ˈdeth \ :

1: the end of life
2: the cause of loss of life
3: a cause of ruin
4: the state of being dead
5: destruction, extinction the death of the dinosaurs
6: slaughter[ix]

Power noun, \ ˈpau̇(-ə)r \

1: ability to act or produce an effect
2: possession of control, authority, or influence over others[x]

Them pronoun \ (th̲)əm

1: Those individuals under discussion: the ones previously mentioned or referred to.
2: Unspecified persons

Fourth noun \ ˈfȯrth \ 1: One that is number four in a countable series.

Beasts noun \ ˈbēst \

1: a four-footed mammal
2: a contemptible person

If we were to look back at the annals of world history, we would all agree upon one fact; that there is only one race of people who fit these definitions. Pale is defined as 3:

not dark or intense in hue, this comes from lack of melanin in your skin—making your skin complexion white/pale. We are taught that white skin complexion or people having this deficiency, comes from grafting or separating the two germs (dominant gene, or the Black germ and the recessive gene or the Brown germ). Then grafted the brown germ into its weakest stage by destroying all traits of the Black germ—EUGENTICS! Thus this is what and how the pale skin nations of Europe was made.

The second line of Revelation 6:8 reads: *And the name of him who sat on it was Death, and Hell followed with him.*

This means that the mentality that sat on the mind of Europeans, is a mentality of Death, and every parcel of the planet Earth that the European has put his foot on—Hell has followed, and the original people of that land has caught Hell.

Q. What are the mental and physical powers of a real devil?

A. The mental power of a devil is nothing in comparison to that of the original man. He only has 6 oz. of brain, while the original man has 7 ½ oz. of brain. The devil is weak boned and weak because he is grafted from the original man. The devil's physical power is 1/3 less than that of the original man. Therefore, his mental and physical power is much less than that of the original man.

The unlearned might say, "How did the Caucasian white man become a dominant ruler in the land if his mental and physical powers is less than the original mans'? Because it was predicted that the Caucasian white race shall rule for a set time by means of with the trickknowledge that was taught to them. The white race was given 6,000 years to rule by force, famine, destruction and racism. However, his rulership expired in the year 1914 A.D, so whoever is still under the domination of the Caucasian white man, is so by his own free will; because they "love" the devil because the devil gives them nothing. Our people has lost the knowledge of ourselves, civilization, righteousness, the science of everything in life, and the moral principles of love, peace and happiness. Because we have ate the wrong foods, we have become other than our own selves.

The original people make up a fourth of the Earth's population. In any pact, in any land mass you go to, you will find an original man, woman and child. At the time of the devil's expiration date, the original people numbered the white man 11 to 1—4,400,000 original people to 400,000 white people.

The system of racism created by the Caucasian white man, is a self-refueling, diabolical and human devouring beast that no one is able to make war with, because no one is like unto the beast.

WHAT IS THE BEAST?

We have been taught by slave makers of the poor, a spook-out version of the Holy Qur'an and Bibl. El Hajj Malik El Shabazz (Malcom X) once said: "Only a fool would let his enemy educate his children."

The Holy Qur'an and the Bible is the history of the original man, the Supreme Being Black man of Asia. But because our legacy was stolen by identity thieves, we have been made to believe that the pale skin race of Europe is in fact the original people of the Holy Qur'an and the Bible, and we; the black, brown, red and yellow aborigines are products of a Hamitic curse. Racists' filmmakers always make movies about biblical times depicting the white race as the original inhabitants of the land. Black people make up the majority of the moviegoers nationwide, and we never question the truthfulness of these movies. We always take the devils' word of face value.

Although America's system of racism is described as a 'Beast', what it really is, is a cannibalistic "MACHINE". This is the very reason Alabama coined itself as "THE MACHINE". Alabama became the life line of the Confederate South, the vital organ that pumped racism through the entire S.E.C. This is why Alabama is called the "Heart of Dixie".

Once agreed upon, the delegates called for a constitutional conventional in the spring of 1901. All the representatives met in Montgomery to come up with a stratagem that would codify old methods and views with new laws that would efficiently render blacks as second-class citizens.

The delegate first attack was on the voting rights. By making Jim Crow the law of the land, 60% of Alabama's Black population became disenfranchised. With voting rights restrictions and de Jure Segregation, The

Redeemers, were able to solidify white supremacy throughout the State of Alabama. Although a large number of blacks were affected by this new constitution, the ripple effect of this BEAST was that it disenfranchised more lower class white citizens than blacks. Even with the loop holes for these poor whites, by 1941-42 over 500,000 whites were not allowed to vote.

The 1901 constitution vilest accomplishment was the rebirthing of the Alabama order of the Ku Klux Klan. The 1901 constitution stood for all the things that made Alabama the most racist state in the south, and this new Order of the Christian Knights (Ku Klux Klan) enforced all of its prejudice news and laws. The Klan grew from a southern brotherhood faction, to a nationwide cult.

If we examine any major company in America that manufacture good on a mass scale, we would find that those company's most valuable asset is not the product which it sells, but the machine that produces the product. Employees are always supplemental, and can be replaced without any money lost. But to maintain and keep the machine operational, it takes money and a lot of it.

Slavery has always been a fortune 500 business, and its machine, the Peculiar Institutions, i.e., ghettoes, schools, law enforcement agencies, courts and prisons are its means of wealth.

Black people in American pay the maintenance cost to keep this slave making machine running at every level. We pay to live in their projects and government houses. We pay to send our children to their schools, to become their minimum wage workers. We pay taxes for policies to have them come into our communities and kill our Black men and children. We pay court cost and ticket fines when we're racially profiled an illegally pulled over and served with bogus tickets; and then we pay "sell-out" lawyers in criminals case.

Last, B-U-T not at all least, we always pay to keep ourselves locked-up by spending our family members (mostly our grandmothers, mothers, aunts, and female companions) money on their commissaries and buying packages two and three times a year. We also contribute to their parasitic system by providing free labor on their plantations, just like slavery and the convict leasing system.

In 1901, blacks made up over forty percent of Alabama's population. However, the constitutional convention was held by all whites in Montgomery; and consisted of 150 delegates in which 96 of the 150 were lawyers. Their jobs was to systematically craft White Supremacy into the state grand-body of law without the Supreme Court noticing any discrepancies.

The convention of 1901 reminds me of the Hampton Court Conference that was held on January 14-16 in 1604. It was at this illegally and secretly held convention that 54 scholars under the order of King James crafted New English/White Supremacy version of the Bible. With a motion by a racist bigot, Dr. John Reynolds, who at that time, was the president of Corpus Christi College, Oxford and leader of the Puritan Party, these so-called scholars, who one namely was William <u>Shake</u> (PSALM 46, count 46 words down) <u>Spear</u> (count 46 words upward), revised the biblical text to better suit Anglo-Saxons.

Q. Why does the devil keep our people apart from his own social equality?

A. Because he doesn't want us to know how filthy he is in all of his affairs. He is afraid that once we learn about him, we will run him from among us. Social means to advocate a society of men or group of men for one common cause. Equality means to be equal in everything.

As was noted earlier, there was no person of Afrikan descent in the 1901 convention for this fact, the principle these of the convention was white supremacy, and everyone in attendance expressed this viewpoint boldly. The word Devil is a derivative of Diablo, or diablos in Latin and Greek which means Slanderer.

During the convention, the delegates made it transparent that their main objective was to disenfranchise Afrikans from their social equality. To quote every racist slander that was made doing the convention would overprint my writing, B-U-T to prove just now "diabolical", the Devil really is in all his affairs, the following slanderous statements was made by some of the delegates doing the convention.

> "I am persuaded that some short message should be delivered to this convention by one of these younger men and one who has never known slavery. I mean slavery as it existed prior to the war, because so far I

am concerned, and we of the younger generation, we have known but one slavery, and that salves to the negro vote, and when I say this I mean it in its fullest and deepest sense, for if there ever was a set of people-slaves to the votes of an unprogressive race; slaves to the slaves of our own fathers, the hardest task-masters that ever drew the blood of life from a quivering nation. Not slaves in a physical sense indeed, but even worse, for while we of the Caucasian race are held responsible for the policy and politics of this county, yet those of the North, not understanding that they have thrown upon us a vote—a vote that is harder to bear than the lash of the cruel task-master… I say here without fear of contradiction that if there is any good in the Negro race—such as elevates a nation, or elevates his race—I say that good comes from the Caucasian blood that runs in his veins." ~ Gesner Williams of Marengo County.

"In the course of time, gentlemen of the convention, the slaves were hunted out in Africa. The Negro wandering through the woods like a beast of the field, and brought here to do what (?). Put upon the block and sold to the highest bidder, to be the servant of his superior, the white man in this county. I believe as truly as I believe that I am standing here, that God Almighty intended the Negro to be the servant of the white man. I believe that the scripture will sustain my position on that question. I know he's inferior to the white man and I believe that delegates of this convention believe him to be. He knows it himself."

"The striking from (the Negro) of the title of slave, and placing in his hand the ballot was the most diabolical piece of tyranny ever visited upon a proud though broken people,"

I would just as soon give a toddling child a razor in his hand, expecting him not to hurt himself, as to expect the Negro to use the ballot and not use it to his injury and to ours," and "God Almighty has made them different from the white man. You had just as well try to legislate a donkey into an Arabian courser, as to legislate a Negro into a white man. You cannot do it. It is impossible to do it." ~ Thomas Heflin, Chambers County.

It was these beliefs and sentiments of all 150 delegates that influence the 1901 constitution which made white supremacy and the law cognates. There has always been ordinance i.e., slave codes, black codes and Jim Crow laws that have dictated the relationship between Afrikans and Caucasians/Blacks and Whites. However, a state's constitution is its grand law above all laws, and when it becomes grafted by mixing, diluting and tampering with it, and is no longer in its original intent; then that "State" becomes weak and wicked. This is why Alabama is on record as being the "last state to free its slaves".

When the war ended and the 13th Amendment was added to the U.S. Constitution, southern states was furious by this behestment. The operation of chattel slavery wasn't abolished by the 13th Amendment, only the sole proprietorship of slavery was under this new system. Slavery became a legal corporate enterprise ran by the government and the states. In Alabama, just 26 years after the war, black made up over 60% of an Alabama's prison population.

John Rogers of Sumter County when addressing the floor had this to say about corporal punishment of black inmates:

> Now everybody knows that the great bulk of convicts in this state are Negroes. Everybody who knows anything about the character of Negro, knows that there is no punishment in the world that can take the place of the lash with him. He must be controlled that way. He inherited that peculiarity from his ancestors when he *came from the shores of Africa* where they provide that kind of punishment, and if we take away the lash from this convict system, we will destroy the efficiency of the system.

I would debate that the 1901 Constitution was the spark that ignited the School Prison Pipeline in Alabama. My reasons for asserting this is because the 1901 Constitution specifically targeted Black children educational opportunities. They did this by first disenfranchising Black public schools from Whites, then levying property taxes for school funding and thirdly, disapportionly those founds to all-white schools.

The 1901 articles had the same racist intent as those of the 1875. In fact, the Apportionment Act was re-enacted in the Constitution of 1901. What spur the S.TO.P.P system is when Afrikan children are inadequately educated in a white neocolonial system, which doesn't have any intention or producing equal and successful competitors in the global economic market. To confirm this fact, Thomas Heflin, also known as "Cotton Tom", had this to say during the convention:

> The Negroes are being educated very rapidly, and I say…someday, when the two separate and distinct races are thrown together, someday the clash will come and only the fittest will survive, and I do not believe it is incumbent upon us to lift him up and educate him and put him on an equal footing that he may be armed and equipped when the combat comes.

When most people, especially Afrikan people think of racism, we usually think of acts of violence or derogatory comments. We rarely ever look at it from a Genocide vs. Survival standpoint. With Black children improperly educated, and living far below the proposed poverty line, plus with the influx of drugs, alcohol and guns facilitated by the systems, Black children are easily lead in the wrong direction, and hard to be lead in the right. Although Black females often fall within this system, the school to prison pipeline is by design aimed at young Afrikan males. Just by looking at the dispirited population of these modern-day plantations, one might assume that Black people commit more crimes than any other race, esp, more than the White race of America. However, this crime statistics report conducted by the Federal Bureau of Investigation, U.S. Dept. of Justice, shows that White people committed more crimes than Black people in every category except two (see chart. Arrests by Race, 2010).

*Imprisonment rate by gender, race, Hispanic origin, & age 2009

On the reverse side, the chart labeled Imprisonment Rate by Gender, Race, Hispanic Origin, and age, 2009, shows two contentions which proves the declarative of this book. First, it exposes the paradox shift between the two charts. Chart A shows more white more whites being arrested. Chart B shows the contradicting factor of more Blacks being imprisoned. The other point is the overall intention of the system. These charts provide conclusive evidence that not only Alabama, B-U-T AmeriKKKa is Just-ICE when it comes to her Afrikan citizens.

To further prove that America feels justified when it targets Just-US, the last chart labeled "Hate crimes by offense Type, Bias Motivation, 2009" shows that there are more Anti-Black crimes committed than anti-white. This isn't new news for conscious Black people. Whenever, wherever a courtroom door opens up, we know that that day an Asiatic Black person will be publicly lynched because Black Lives don't matter in courtrooms.

WHAT IS "CIVIL RIGHTS" WITHOUT HUMANE TREATMENT?

According to Scott Foresman Intermediate Diction, Civil Rights is defined as:

1) The rights of a citizen, especially the rights guaranteed to all U. S. citizens regardless of race, color, religion, or sex.

Understanding this, we must examine the two essential amendments of the constitution which qualifies as person as a citizen.

Amendment II. A well-regulated militia, being necessary to the security of a free state, the right of the people to keep and bear arms shall not be infringed.

Amendment XV. Section 1. The right of citizens of the United States to vote shall not be denied or abridged by the United States or by any state of account of race, color or previous condition of servitude.

The 2nd Amendment grants a person the right to keep and bear arms as necessary for securing freedom through a well-regulated militia.

Reviewing the history of America and her intercourse with Black people, the only thing worse than giving a Black person a gun is giving him a book and teaching him how to read. The first 10 Amendments of the constitution are called "The Bill of Rights" and was written in 1791, in a scope of time when Black people in America didn't have any rights; nor considered human enough to attain citizenship.

We must ask ourselves, "Why is the 2nd Amendment one of the only two Amendments taken after the 13th Amendment has remanded its subjects?". Even if a person is convicted of a non-violent crime or property crime which doesn't involve a weapon, these two Amendments (2nd and 15th) are still retracted in their sentence exceed one year. So why is the 2nd Amendment retracted? It is because slaves are not permitted to have a gun. Why? Because in our repressive state, we tend to turn our aggression towards our oppressors. A perfect example of this and the fear it caused is the Black Panther Party of the 60s, 70s and early 80s. Because they were educated and armed, the Black Panther Party became the greatest threat (Public Enemy #1) to the white power status quo.

The key to understanding the 2nd Amendment is to breakdown its meaning and examine its core purpose.

1) Well-regulated, adv. - In a legally sufficient manner; unobjectionable.
   1) To control or direct in agreement with a rule.
   2) To adjust in conformity to a requirement or specification.
2) Militia, n. - A military force that is not part of a regular army.
   1) The whole body of physically fit male civilians eligible by law for military service.
   2) A body of citizens armed and trained, esp. by a state, for military purpose. "…being necessary to the security of as."
3) Free state, n. - A state governed as an autonomous (self-ruling) political unit under international auspices (protection or support).

To interpret the 2nd Amendment in light most favorable to its implied intent.

A well-regulated militia would mean: a society of men or group of men who are armed and trained for one common cause which would be protecting and securing the rulership of a white supremacy enterprise within its national borders. Therese groups or societies are the racist hate groups that has plague Afrikan people ever since the days of their predecessors, the Crusades, Ku Klux Klan, Confederate Conservative Citizens, skinheads, Ayran Brotherhoods, and so forth. All of these "cults" are backed by the National Rifle Association (NRA) of America. Which, as of this date, has over four million members, members who make up all of the terrorist groups I just mentions.

Another reason why the second amendment is retracted is because if and when whites decide to wage civil war on blacks, a large percentage of black people between the ages of 16-49 are procedurally barred from owning a weapon, black people as a whole would be defenseless, and just as lame sheep amongst a pack of wolves. A perfect example of this is the Stand Your Ground Law/(SYG), which justifies white people killing Blacks and Latinos simply because they "feel" threaten.

Just think, what if someone inside of the Emanuel African Methodist Episcopal AME Church in Charleston, South Carolina was armed with a pistol when white racist assassin, Dylann Roof, came in and murdered nine beautiful Christians. If someone was "packin" that Yacob's grafted devil would not have killed as many people as he did before someone would have busted a cap in his ass!

Ever since 1865, America has enacted double-standard laws which have justified its illegal entrapment of people of Afrikan descent. An example of this double-standard is stated in the 2nd Amendment that "the right of the people to keep and bear arms <u>shall not be infringed.</u> Then executing a provision that if "a person of the said people is convicted, and his/her sentence exceeds one year, then they cannot "keep and bear arms". We know that this web of hypocrisy catches people of all races, however, if you would research, the number of 3x-felons convicted under the U.S. I.C.E. Law (Isolating the criminal element). I guarantee you that more blacks are convicted every year than whites. The reason being is that 90% of black people that is released from these modern-day slave plantations are thrown back into the same poverty-burden neighborhoods. Neighborhoods that are purposely infested with drugs, hustlers, gangs, and of course, guns. With the proclivity for survival implanted within the psyche of these newly-freed slaves, arming one's self with a gun becomes second nature. It is at this point that the 5th stage of Mass Incarceration System/Business kicks in. The system of mass incarceration is set up on five stages of factors; 1) Under education, 2) Poverty, 3) Criminality, 4) Incarceration and 5) Release and recidivism (re-capturing).

When we hear the words Department of Correction (DOC), most people believe that these institutions were put in place to correct the individual it encages. However, on the contrary, these modernized slave plantations do not "correct", nor do they minimize the criminality of a person. What these peculiar institutions do is so-called correct society, or remove unwanted and unacceptable elements from a civilized demon-cracy. But this notion is folly in its own concept because 1) American was built up and colonized by "criminals", and 2) there will never exist (again) the reality of an "all-white utopias". It is my belief that this "idea" of an "all white America" is the motivation behind the currently industrialize slave system called PRISONS.

Because prisons are not designed to rehabilitate a person nor to change or modify one's behavior, when a young black male comes to prison, he is automatically thrust into a defensive mind set. His frame of thinking is solely "trust no one, watch out for sexual predators, mind your business; I need a knife or weapon". He simultaneously becomes adapted to his environment and focus on all of the things that will keep him save and alive, not on rehabilitating himself. To secure his safety, he will socialize with whatever gang, sub-gang, county or religious set he feels will guarantee this.

What makes the 5th factor of the Mass Enslavement System so effective is that out of the 18 correctional facilities in Alabama, none of them actually promote or implement alternative programs that's geared towards destroying the criminal thinking of a person and building a totally new mind set. All of the Substance Abuse Programs (SAP), which only focus on drug and alcohol, are strictly voluntary. Also, these programs only exist because of the grant money a facility receives from the federal Government. So, since it's not mandatory that a person gets a GED or a trade of skill. *Inmates* become "conform and complaisant" to the interstructure of prisons.

According to a report by the Alabama Justice Department: Alabama Department of correction receives 95 inmates monthly, 75% of adults prisoners return to crime when released, 85% of juvenile prisoners return to crime when released. Out of the 95% of people who go to prison and get out, there's a 160% recidivism rate.

In Alabama's three maximum security prison, there is over 3,400 inmates, with an estimate of 1,100 out of the total population being Caucasian males. Also, 3 out of every 5 Afrikan males that return to prison do so with new cases that involves a gun.

The general assessment by American's so-called criminologists and psychiatrists is that there's a dysfunction in the thinking ability of Black males which is why so many return to crime after they're released from prison. Although there's no facts backing this up, when most Black males return to prison, many are evaluated and diagnosed as having some sort of metal disorder. They are then placed on what is called a case file. This is because for every person deemed as "a mental health prisoner", that person gets extra money for his or her treatment; which they never get.

Because this is a multi-billion dollar business, the real reason why most Black males return to prison is never discussed. That will be like throwing rocks and "not" hiding your hands. In fact, the very reason why Blacks return to prison is the reason why they commit crimes and go to prison the first time—Aggravating Circumstances.

According to BLACK LAW DICTIONARY, aggravating circumstances is; 1) A fact or situation that increases the degree of liability of culpability for a criminal act 2) A fact or situation that relates to a criminal offense of a defendant and that is considered by the court in imposing punishment.

El Hajj Malik El Shabazz (Malcom X) once said, "They sell us the liquor, then lock us up for being drunk."

Through aggravating circumstances, meaning orchestrating or manipulating and creating an environment or atmosphere feasible for crime, one can mathematically calculate how man, Black males and females, out of an associated group will end up in jail or prison.

In these (neighborhoods) called ghettos which by standard American Dictionary meaning is a section of a city, esp. 2) thickly populated slum area, inhabited predominantly by Negroes, Puerto Ricans or any other minority group, often as a result of social and economic restrictions. Out of this "economic restrictions", which is just a fancy word for poverty, spring forth crime.

In the book, "The BLUEPRINT" OF A New Concept, by Roderick L. Emery. Sr. In chapter 4 (pp 38-39), under the heading THE AWAKENING, he gives a rationale view of the everyday reality of these "HOODS".

> Our lifestyle is a reaction to an environmental condition, the Ghetto. The Ghetto with its vices,

overcrowdings and unending insanity, provides an enticing place for crime of all sorts.

The Ghetto throws desperate and unhappy people into an unbearable closeness, thereby increasing potential frictions, giving birth to never-ending quarrels of accusation and vindictiveness which produces "gangbanging" personalities. Black on Black crime is on the rise. Drug addiction is epidemic, incurable diseases (AIDS and Herpes) have become common and chaos is everywhere.

While all the above is going on, we are forces to witness the controllers of this land being caught in **lies** of fraud and deceit, biocide (the destruction of our children) fratricide (Brother killing Brother), homicide and genocide. The TOTAL destruction of a race of group of people has become the "order" of the day.

The Ghetto concentrates these pressures and tensions and injects them into our individual personalities causing most of us to become opportunistic, parasitic and exploitive of our own kind.

The mass incarceration of Black people and other people of melanianethnicity is a multi-billion dollar business. In every Afrikan and Hispanic neighborhood, you will always find an abundance of class-A narcotics, i.e., cocaine (crack), heroin, methamphetamine and marijuana. Because this is a national corporation, with multiple stockholders, every entity must benefit from the self-destructing dealings of the perpetrator. On the bottom level, you have the "supplier", whether he be white or black. This is the person that sells large quantities of narcotics to the person that's a little higher than a street dealer.

Although there isn't enough courtroom evidence to prove that the U.S. Government has its hands directly in the drug network, however, there has been documented records that states that American has allowed tons of narcotics to enter her boarders, and has flooded the neighborhoods of Afrikan and Hispanics people for "political reason". (Freeway Rick Ross)

On the 2nd level, you have your local law enforcement agency. Because these "Ghettos and Projects" are high crime risks, polices are always getting government funding for new equipment, cars, bonuses for the more Afrikan and Hispanics they arrest, extra money for sting operations, and rewards for how many they send to prison.

However, before any attempt to initiate a drug bust, law enforcement agencies allow the drug trade to operate for a while. The reason for this is to allow the dealer to accumulate enough money so that they can spend it with the rich ruling class. This is one of the ways that companies that have stock or money invested in the prison industrial business get their money. They watch while they spend it on clothes that's made by the rich ruling class, buy jewelry, expensive shows, cars and rims that's manufactured by the rich ruling class, and go to clubs and buy alcoholic drinks. They know that they're going to do everything with the money they make off the destruction of their people and neighborhoods, except build up their communities and start businesses for the empowerment of their people. So this is why law enforcements agencies let a drug operation run for months, sometimes for years before thy make a drug bust.

After they feel that the dealer has gotten enough "Big Bucks", that's when the 3rd level starts to get paid. The third level is the judicial system which consists of county sheriff departments, bail bondsmen, lawyers and court costs and of course the judge gets paid for every conviction. The forth level is the prison (slavery) system which makes millions on top of millions of dollars off of free labor of incarcerated citizen.

People always ask the questions. How do we stop this genocidal system, what's the solution?

Before I give them a direct answer, I explain to them, to the pint or era in time in which we lost focus of the reason(s) we were protesting at first. We neglect to recall the overall goal and reward we were seeking. That was independent liberation, and not a subservient freedom.

Independent liberation is the owning and controlling of our political avenues, our economical and educational systems, and all private and public entities, right down to the local police departments.

During reconstruction, Blacks flocked to the political arena to make these plans materialize, which they did in places like Tulsa, OK and Baltimore, MD. It wasn't until we allowed certain "people", whom the majority of them looked just like us, but wasn't with us, come amongst us and define to us what we wanted and what was "freedom".

It's documented facts that every organization, every moment we ever had has been infiltrated by agents provocateurs. When we came out of chattel slavery, we had aims of owning our farm lands, businesses, and schools; but in the midst of the civil rights movements, 'someone' changed our theme from "Black own" to integration!

As a race of people, we knew that the doorway to independent liberation was the power of the baton. The unrestrictive ability to select leaders that will honestly, sincerely and fearlessly represent us in our totality. Not to confuse my notion with today's privileges and poly-tricks. When I say independent liberation, I'm speaking of complete sovereignty; being self-governed under the principles of family, God and love.

In today's political circus, black interest is last on the list. No one, not even the Negro governors and mayors we so enthusiastically vote for represent Afrikan Diaspora people here in the wilderness of North America. This is a country that in her early development, told her mother, that there will be "NO TAXATION, WITHOUT REPRESENTATION". That meant that if you don't represent us in our best interest, we want pay tribute and homage to you, we want obey your laws, and we will not spend our money with you. It was through this resolution and defiance that America became an independent country. Not only America, but here was several Afrikan populated states and countries that gained their independency by "STANDING UP" and saying "NO MORE". Only the American Negro became fragmented and mislead and also tricked into believing that we have gain true freedom.

Malcom X said, THE BALOT OR THE BULLET, two powers that is taken from millions of Black people once reverted back into slavery. Citizenship depends on these two abilities which are fundamental rights under the Constitution of this said government. Without these two rights, you are powerless, defenseless and thus a "Negro" or a "Poor White Trash".

The right to vote means the ability to change these unjust laws, laws which were written during a time when racism ran wild and white supremacy ruled every aspect of Black people lives. Alabama's 1901 Constitution is by far the most prejudice doctrine ever written and an unadulterated symbol of Hate. Within its context lies "THE BIRTH of a NATION," "THE MISEDUCATION of a NEGRO," GENTRIFICATION BY TAXATION and "THE DESTRUCTION of a BLACK civilization". Because the 1901 Constitution is still in its original form, Jim Crow still lives, The Black Codes are still prevalent and white supremacy is still the face of Alabama.

IV

New Slavery:

Black Men in Prison

A: Facts and Statistics

Prisons discord the unity amongst incarcerated citizens and love ones. It separates a son or daughter from their mother and father, a husband from his wife and children, causes financial instability and emotional distress; and once again destroys the black male image of a household.

In Michel Foucault's *DISCIPLINE AND PUNISH: The Birth of Prison*, he explains the transition of torture from a public and physical operation to a hidden and external functioning.

Similarly, the hold on the body did not entirely disappear in the mid-nineteenth century. Punishment had no doubt ceased to be centered on torture as a techniques of pain; it assumed as its principal object loss of wealth or gifts. But a punishment like forced labour or even imprisonment - mere loss of liberty – has never functioned without a certain additional element of punishment that certainly concerns the body itself: rationing of food, sexual deprivation, corporal punishment, solitary confinement. Are these the unintentional, but inevitable consequence of imprisonment?

In fact, in its most explicit practices, imprisonment has always involved a certain degree of physical pain. The criticism that was often levelled at the penitentiary system in the early ninetieth century (imprisonment is not a sufficient punishment: prisoners are less hungry, less cold, less deprived in general than many poor people or even workers) suggests a postulate that was never explicitly denied: it is just that a condemned man should suffer physically more than other men. It is difficult to dissociate punishment from additional physical pain.

What would a non-corporal punishment be?

There remains, therefore, a trace of 'torture' in the modern mechanisms of criminal justice – trace that has not been entirely overcome, but which is enveloped, increasingly, by the non-corporal nature of the penal system.

If the penalty in its most sever forms no longer addressed itself to the body, on what does it lay hold? The answer of the theoreticians-those who- (about 1760), open up a new period that is not yet at an end-is simple, almost obvious. It seems to be contained is the question itself: since it is no longer the body, it must be the "soul". The expiation that once rained down upon the body must be replaced by a punishment that acts in depth on the heart, the thoughts, the will, and the inclinations.

Mably formulated the principle once and for all: Punishment, if I may so put it, should strike the soul rather than the body. (Mably, 326)

Alabama's prisons were built to house an estimate of 14,000 inmates, the actual capacity is 13,318. In July 2016, Alabama's in-house population was 23,692. That's 1,438 women, 22,254 men. ADOC is now operation at almost double the capacity. The most overcrowded high security large men's facility is Kilby Correctional, at 266 percent capacity in July. That's 1,169 inmates in a space designed to hold 440 inmates. The number to correctional employees at Kilby is 141, that's about 60% the recommended correctional staff level.

According to the National Institute of Correction, in 2013, Alabama's incarceration rate was 64 & higher than the national average of adults in prison per every 100,000 residents. Alabama rate was 647 while the national average was 395. Also, a report prepared by the Center on Budget and Policy Priorities, showed that the incarceration rate in Alabama has risen by 349% between 1978 and 2013. The national average for the same timeframe was 250%.

According to a Decennial Census Result, done by the U.S. Census Bureau; conducted in 2010 and 2013, Blacks make up 26.2% of Alabama's population, whites make up the majority, 68.5% in Alabama's Department of Corrections. (Industrialized Slaver Corporation). Blacks make up a vastly 68.2% of the total population. One out of every three Black males age 23 to 38 are in prison, jail, or on probation or parole. This proves that slaver was never abolished, and that the fate of young Black males is still in the hands of our open oppressors. Also, according to the Prison Policy Initiative from the U.S. Census Bureau, a summary prepared in 2010 showed that the rate of Black inmates was three times higher than the number of white inmates incarcerated in all types of correctional facilities within the state. Those facilities include federal, state, local jails, halfway houses and community corrections facilities.

The summary reported that 535 out of every 100,000 white residents were incarcerated. Similarly, 767 out of every

100,000 Hispanic residents and 1,788 out of every 100,000 Black residents were incarcerated in one of the types of correctional facilities across the state. According to the 2014 annual report from the ADOC, the state's correctional facilities are dangerously overcrowded. The overall occupancy rate, expressed as a calculation of the number of inmates divided by the number of designed capacity beds, far exceeds the occupancy rate each facility was designed for.

Jail system

Alabama has 67 counties according to the surveys done in 2013 and 20104, there are 110 jails and adult detainment facilities with a population of 15,612.

The Prison System

As of December 31, 2014, the Alabama prison population was 31,1771. In FY2014 (Fiscal Year), the ADOC employed a staff of 3,878 in 16 major correctional facilities; and community based facilities The Budget for FY2014 was $448 million.

Community Correction

The Alabama Broad of Pardons and Parole supervised 53,839 probationers and 10,374 parolees through 62 field offices through the state in FY2014. The daily cost of supervising an offender through 62 field offices was $2.31.

Alabama has a rate about 2% lower than the national average number of probationers per 100,000 people.

Taxpayers in Alabama paid about 46 & lower than the other states per inmate in 2012.

Alabama's incarceration rate is rank 5th worst in the world.

Alabama rate is only topped by Louisiana, Mississippi, and Oklahoma; and represents one of the only 5 states in the Union with an incarceration rate higher than 600 adults in prison per every 100,000 residents.

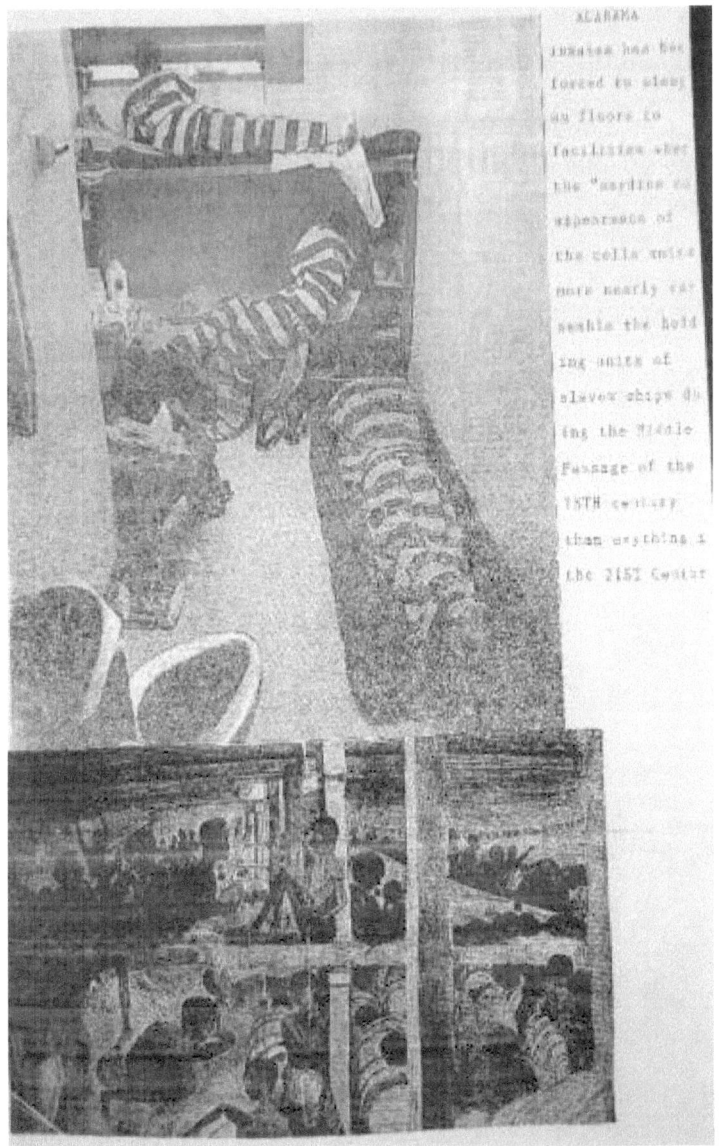

ALABAMA inmates has bee forced to sleep on floors in facilities wher the "sardine ca appearance of the cells unite more nearly rea semble the hold ing units of slaves ships du ing the Middle Passage of the 18TH century than anything i the 21ST Centur

Q: Is the American Justice System Fair and Just to Melanianated People?

This is a question I want you to ask yourself and answer. The guaranteed rights within the 5th and 6th Amendment are the essential and mandatory requirements for ta just criminal justice system.

Amendment V

"No person shall be held to answer for a capital or otherwise infamous crime, unless on a presentment of indictment of a grand jury, except in cases arising in the land or naval forces, or in the militia, when in actual service in time of war or public danger; (2) nor shall any person be subject for the same offense to be twice put in jeopardy of life or limb; (3) nor shall be compelled in any criminal case to be a witness against himself; (4) nor be deprived of life, Liberty, or property, without due process of law, nor shall private property be taken from public use, without just compensation.

  ELEMENTS

  1) Presentment/Indictment
  2) Double Jeopardy
  3) Right against self-incrimination
  4) Due Process

The first underlined clause refers to a presentment or indictment which is a written accusation of a crime made by a grand jury and presented to a court for prosecution against the accused person. Before you are tried and punished for a crime, the grand jury must first find probable cause to believe you are guilty of the accusation presented din the indictment. If the grand jury returns with the True bill that means that a criminal charge should go before a petty jury for trial. If they return a No bill, this means that the court does not have enough evidence to prosecute the accused person. Because Alabama is a prison industrial state, its very rare that a grand jury in any county would issue a No bill. In fact, over 43 percent of Alabama's convicted citizens have been convicted or manipulated into pleading guilty to a crime in which there was little or no evidence to uphold a conviction. Also, out of the 43%, Black made up the vast majority at 29%.

Though out America, according to The National Registry of Exonerations, of the

1050 individual exonerations from January 1989 through December 201: 93.2% were men (979/1050) and 6.7% were women (71/1050).

    47.3% were black (485/1025),
    38.5 % were white (395/1025),
    12.2% were Hispanic (126/1025, and
     1.8% were Native American or Asian (19/1025)

The Double Jeopardy clause protects you from being charged with the same crime twice, but you can be charged with two offenses arising from one crime.

When the crack epidemic reached middle-class suburban neighborhoods, it became a national problem instead of being just a "poor Black problem".

Congress passed anti-crack laws with the approval of the Reagan administration and his "war on crime" Campaign. This allowed federal and state officials to raid crack houses and charged dealers with the multiple counts for the same incident, thus making them habitual offender; which gave rise to the "three strikes, and you're out" Law.

With this leverage, the state of Alabama has devised another diabolic scheme to legally genocide the Afrikan family and poor white Alabamians. Over 1300 Alabama prisoners are now serving sentences of life imprisonment without the possibility of parole. According to a report issued by the Sentencing Project, Alabama (population 4.5 million) ranks third in the nation, behind California (35.5 million) and New York (19.1 million). In the percentage of its prison population serving sentences of Life and Life Without Parole.

An important clause within the 5th Amendment is the self-incrimination clause. Since 2012, there have been 39 guilty-plea exonerations in the last 4 years. That's almost 10 exoneration per year. In the majority of these cases, innocent people was either threaten or coerced into accepting plea bargains rather than risk higher penalties at trial.

Every day the so-called *justice system* entraps countless of innocent civilians, all before they are cleared do nonreciprocal amount of the time; half for at least 9 years or more, about 75% for at least 4 years. There was a time when confrontation with law enforcement officers meant "I plead the fifth (5th)", now because our environment make us feel as though- "The color of our skin is a crime", we tend to cooperate with the authority even when we don't have to. The Due Process Clause protects a citizen against non-compliance with the fundamental rules for a fair and "Just" legal proceeding. However, the only way to ensure that your Due Process Clause has not been or have been violated, is to know the Rules of Criminal Procedures. In a court of Law, if you don't understand the "rules of Court", 9 ¾ times out of 10, you'll be wrongfully convicted, or as the saying goes…"You'll be railroaded".

In Alabama, U.S. currency determines what rules the court will play by which means "money walks, and poor people get time on top of time.

AMENDMENT VI

[1]In all criminal prosecutions, the accused shall enjoy the right to a speedy and public trial, by an impartial jury of the state and district wherein the crime shall have been committed, which district shall have been previously ascertained by law, and [2] to be informed of the nature and cause of the accusation, [3] to be confronted with the witness against him; [4] to have compulsory process for obtaining witnesses in his favor, and [5] to have the assistance of counsel for his defense.

ELEMENTS

1) Speedy and public trial and impartial jury
2) Informed of nature and cause of the accusation
3) Confronted by witness
4) Compulsory process/expert witnesses

5) Assistance of counsel

In the art of war, the best strategist and tactician will always win the majority of the battles. The fact that war has been declared on the Black and Brown men in these Hells of North America. There must be a reeducating, a retraining and a rebirthing of the mind-set of our people in order to secure the existence of our people in future times. Our open and avowed enemy sits around in boardrooms, laboratories, in churches and temples, even on "golf courses" and plan our demise.

LEGALLY, the judge's chamber in the meeting place where millions of BLACK LIVES is bargained and traded off like slave auctions doing antebellum times. This bartering is down while the accused person sits idly in confinement for months or years before he/she goes to trial. This waiting process or what is commonly called 'sweating it out', is designed to agitate the accused person and make him impatient, so that he/her will make a rash decision and cop a plea deal.

According to data produced by The National Registry of Exonerations, 95% of felony convictions are the products or guilty pleas. About one-fourth of guilty please come from Involuntary Confessions, in which the police or other law enforcement authorities made promises to coerce or deceive the suspect into confessing to a crime or admitted participation in a crime.

Most defendants enter guilty pleas to receive small sentences and to try to get on with their lives. Although this may be the case, by pleading out, a person 'willfully' revert themselves back into slavery, and become marked property for the rest of their lives, because being convicted is the same as being branded with an insignia of a slave owner to show ownership of his property.

It is well known that a "jury of your peers" doesn't mean that the people who sits in the jury box are qualified to give a thorough attestation of the defendant's character. Most jury pools in criminal cases in Alabama, whereas the defendant is a young to mid-age Black male consist of mostly white jurors in their mid-forties to late sixties. Even with a diverse jury pool, because of the disparagement within Black communities, it is virtually impossible to select a juror whom can relate to the discriminatory factors that plague Black men.

What I mean by this is, because of the systematize function of Black neighborhoods, i.e., underemployment or none at all, under housing, high drop-out rate, drugs etc. And the fact that most people living in these communities has had some sort of run-in with the law. It's rare to find a person that's qualified for jury duty in these neighborhoods. So that eliminates any one that could actually understand why Black men do some of the things they do. There is a saying amongst inmates that contemplate on going to trial…

> You only have 13 ½. That's one judge, twelve jurors, and half (1/2) of chance.

The facts, evidence, and the probable cause as to why the crime was committed, how it was done, and who actually did it; is what is meant by "the nature and cause of the accusation."

(Element) If someone is willing to testify against you, or becomes a snitch and starts telling the police or other law officials about a crime or a "suspected" drug operation, the 6th Amendment gives you the right to confront that person and to attest to the allegation being made. Also, it allows you to obtain witnesses in your favor for your defense.

(Element) Another right encompassed in the 6th Amendment is the right to have the assistance of counsel for your defense. A fair and just criminal justice system requires competent and effective lawyers. In Alabama, there is no statewide indigent defender system. Of the 41 judicial circuits in Alabama, only 4 have a system for public defenders, and only tries capital cases. Then of the 41 circuits hire attorneys for a monthly fee. According to reposts done by a legal research group, in the these counties; the public defender did not file a single motion in 75% of all felony cases, and did not ask of expert witnesses nor additional funds for investigator in 99.4% of all cases.

Alabama state law only sets one requirement for attorneys in capital cases, "that the lawyer only needs five years of criminal experience. Without legal assistance in post-conviction, inmates with no recourse and no funds to investigate beyond prison walls must rely on "Jailhouse Lawyers" or their own inexperience to maneuver through the strenuous requirements of Alabama's Post conviction Remedy, or Rule 32. Many inmates become procedural barred for not complying with the technical requirements of a Kule 32.

If a lawyer do not file a Direct Appeal timely, an inmates only has one year "after" direct appeal to file a Rule 32. If this process does not occur, then the inmate is deemed barred, which may means spending the rest of his life behind bars. Because effective post-conviction representation requires reading the trial transcript, which may contain over a thousand pages; meeting with the client; conducting a detailed investigation, and researching and writing twenty page petitions, attorneys who represent inmates in post convictions and on Rule 32 proceedings always skip or leave out important factors which can possibly free their client.

If Alabama doesn't solve their public defender problem, poor defendants and inmates will never have quality representation in any stage of the criminal process, and the underfunding and ineffectiveness of counsel in Alabama will hinder the ability of the criminal justice system to relinquish fair and just results.

With so many Black and Brown males incarcerated, and so many of our women left alone to maintain the household; our women becomes easy prey for the rich slave-makers of the poor. This separation, which was a prime factor in the Willie Lynch slave manufacturing system, forces our women to become dependent on an anti-minority government. The system creates a financial impoverishment by reducing our females to subsidiary residents in section 8 (government funded housing projects), and making them abide by their do's and don'ts or suffer the consequences.

In a lot of cases, Black females often solicit themselves just to make ends meet. When this happens, the blame is thrown back and forth like a childish game of 'Hot Potations'. She blames him for her hardship because he got 'locked up', he blames her for not being faithful and supportive. Disagreements turn into arguments, arguments turn into separation, and in the end—they both fall 'victim to the system.' This clash not only eradicates the interstructure of a family, it also destroys the Black male image and minimizes the positive cultural influence in the community.

As a nation crawling out of the murky economical system of chattel slavery, the Black Codes, Jim Crow degradation; and the Pimp/Hustler and Gangster glamorization eras, we are still reminded by the profiteers of this unforgotten past every time we wake up and have to struggle just to survive and provide for our families. Alabama's reluctance puts her at the forefront of all the confederate states, because of her refusal to relinquish her views and position in regards to her African male citizen, and their status as a human being and man.

In perpetuating this Interloping Negative, in which the African male has become entrapped in at his earliest and most vulnerable stage of development—his preteens. Certain professional personnel must be in place in order to undermine the mental and physical growth of the young Afrikan child. This tells me that there's a system that has been created and put in place to dumbdown and criminalized young Black boys and girls. In order to assure the success of this system, the system must employ professional agents at every stage of their upbringing and development. This means school teachers, child counselors, childcare resource workers, polices and juvenile social workers and so forth.

When a child starts preschool and kindergarten, his/her natural behavior is energetic, playful and high spirited. However, this joyfulness is often misdiagnosed as some sort of 'unnatural hyperactive disorder; such as ADHD (Attention Deficit Hyperactive Disorder), LD (Learning Disabilities), which is a made up (fictitious) diagnoses. Because most teachers feel as though they're not being paid enough money to attend to the individuality of each student. Most teachers who are hired by the system, self-evaluate the student, and then self-diagnose him or her with one or two of the many fictitious disorder; and then they recommend that the student be given laboratory made drugs and placed in a special education classroom.

Unbeknowing of the critical effects that this decision will have on their child, single mothers are tricked into believing their child has behavior and learning disability, and if they have their child treated (drugged up), that they will receive additional income in the form of "Social Security Disability Income (SSI) checks". The flip side to this is that putting a young child on Ritalin, Prozak and other amphetamine-like drugs do more harm than good. It may solve a short term problem, but statistics show and prove that 75% of children who have been misdiagnosed with one or more of these made-up disabilities, end up committing crimes before the age of 18 for African males, this percentage is even higher considering the fact that only 27% of Black males in 'Special education' classes take these drugs on a daily basis graduate from high school.

In addition to the criminal behavior that a child develops as a result of being "labeled and treated" as a problem child, the physical and psychological side-effects that these depressant drugs have on a child is extremely dangerous. Not only is these psychoactive drugs powerfully addictive, and causes children to develop other addictive habits such as a craving for nicotine (Oxford New Desk Dictionary definition, n. poisonous alkaloid present in tobacco), caffeine (alkaloid drug with stimulant action found in tea leaves and coffee beans.), codeine (analgesic alkaloid from morphine i.e., crack/cocaine) and heroin (highly addictive white crystalline analgesic drug derived from morphine). These pharmaceuticalize drugs also have serious side-effects that causes health problems. Some of the known side side-effects includes antisocial behavior, anxiety, agitation, insomnia; decreased in appetite, nausea, irritability, growth defects, vision impairment and seizures.

So-called 'mental health' inmates make up over half of Alabama's total prison population. That's about 3 out of every 5 inmates contained within the walls of the ADOC.

As I stated earlier, I'm willing to debate the affirmative that the Constitution of 1901 was the spark that ignited Alabama's School to the Prison Pipeline system, and the misdiagnosing and criminalizing of young African males neocolonial schools is the gasoline that keeps it going. Alabama ranks 43 in the nation, at 69.0% when it comes to African male students graduating from high schools. Alabama also has the second highest drop-out rate in the southeast.

A 2010-11 report showed that Alabama incarcerated more African males than it enrolled in colleges during those years. In a recent article printed in the Prison Legal News, which derived it source from a commentary written in the Press Register; a Huntsville, AL. newspaper, it showed how allocation of federal education stimulus funds closely resembles the Apportionment Act of 1891.

Alabama allocated 11% of its federal education stimulus funds to its prison system. Of the $1.1 billion the state received from the U.S. Department of Education from 2009 to 2010, the state gave more than $118 million to the Alabama Department of Corrections (ADOC).

The stimulus money allocated to the ADOC amounts to around $4,500 per prisoner, about four times what is spent on each student in kindergarten through the 12th grade in Alabama.

Considering these figures, one might believe that Alabama's prisons and prisoners are one of the best in the country. 'WRONG'! Alabama spends only $26 per day to incarcerate a prisoner. The national average is more than twice as much, at $62 per inmate. Alabama's per-inmate spending ranks last among 16 states in the southeast where the average daily cost is $40 per inmate. Alabama's prisons have the highest ratio of inmates to correction officers in the county. Unsafe living conditions have been the cause of numerous lawsuits and citations, in which the Supreme Court has ruled that over-crowding in most of Alabama's prisons and local facilities, i.e., county jails, detention centers and halfway houses is 'barbaric and unsafe. With some prison at double the capacity, overcrowded conditions poses substantial health risks to employees and prisoners. When it comes to inmate medical care, Alabama ranks last in the country. The national average per inmate is $7.39, Alabama only spends about $5.50 per inmate. Comparison to all four surrounding states, Alabama leads in prison death rate.

Prisoners die at a rate of 41 deaths per every 10,000 inmates, whereas the national average for all other state prisons in the southeast is 23 deaths per every 10,000 inmates. Since the merger of its parent companies of Correctional Medical Services and PHS Correctional Health care in June 2011, Corizon; the inmate health care provider for Alabama and 30 other states has been the center of over fifty wrongful death lawsuits. Inmate on inmate violence has also become a growing concern because of overcrowding and understaffed condition.

In 2010-12, there were no reports of homicides by the Department of Corrections. However, reports did renew that Alabama Department of Correction reported over 1,397 fights and non-sexual assaults, which was 397 more than it reported in the year before.

At the beginning of the Budget Year (BY) in October 2012, three prisoners were stabbed to death, and since then, the ADOC has reported one more homicides every year. Violence is an everyday occurrence in Alabama's prison system, and one may believe that the most violent acts happen in Alabama's maximum security facilities. 'WRONG AGAIN!"

Instead, the prisons with the highest number of inmate on inmate fights and non-sexual assaults are Alabama's medium and lower level security prisons. Bullock Mental Health facility has the highest reported fights and non-sexual assaults. Other medium level facilities include Draper Correctional Facility, Elmore County Work Released Center, and Bibb County Correctional Facility, which has earned the moniker "Bloody Bill" because of the number of brutal assaults and stabbings. Within prison walls, conflicts are generated by systematic mechanisms design to keep inmates disunified, the same as the principles mentioned in the Willie Lynch Letter.

These subliminal tools is the cause for the cruel and unconstitutional conditions existing inside of Alabama's prison system. Inside the "Belly of the Beast", incarcerated citizens are divided and conquered by a new set of principles. With the same effects as the Slave Making System, these annexation reanimate every scheme that Alabama has ever invented against its African male citizens. These principles are: counties or regions, gangs and cliques, sexuality, ethic or race groups; religion and The Mark system.

Prisons or Plantations not only discord the unification amongst family members and incarcerated love ones, it also subliminally creates an invisible barrier between fellow incarcerated citizens. Prisons are microcosm of every ghetto, trailer park, project and inter-urban neighborhood; which the enslaved person comes from because most reverted slaves where made *deaf, dumb and blind* by the Devil when they were babes, they cannot comprehend the identicalness of antebellum slavery and this now perpetual systematic slavery.

B: The Facts

The "NEGRO STILL IS NOT FREE", even though he believes wholeheartedly in the myth of emancipation, he is still numb to the fact that a needle was stuck in his head, which killed his awareness of who he really is, who God is and who is the Devil with his many plots and schemes.

C: Counties

In Alabama, county conflicts have been the cause of numerous lives wasted. "PRISONERS" argue, fight, and even kill one another over counties which once held their ancestors in slavery. Prisoners or "Properties of the State", go to the extremity to represent these neocolonial counties, by tattooing insolent marks on their body such as "205 Real Niggaz", Gumptown Niggaz", "Hunsvegas Niggaz" and "Mobile Trill Niggaz" and so on. These are the same cities and counties, in the same state that lynched, burned alive, hung, mutilated and sicced Precocious K-9 animals on our parent, grandparents, and great grandparent. This show and prove that the Negro still is not free mentally, spiritually, socially and again physically. Counties

(Prisoners that represent counties) are further divided by gangs and cliques.

D: Gangs and Cliques

These once political activist groups and guardians of our neighborhoods, by and though the influences of governmental operations-FBI Counter Intelligence Program (COINTELPRO). BIG, Brother Watching and Home Land Security have become top priorities on the nations' 'Terrorist Act List. Not because they commit counter insurgency acts like militant Jihadist groups. B-U-T because they have the potential to be the ultimately interior threat to the white supremacy fabric that binds America together. Just like the UNIA, the Black Panther Party and all the other FREEDOM, JUSTICE, and EQUALITY advocacy groups and organization gangs have been infiltrated by nefarious agents of adversary.

Due to the deceptive tactics of an anonymous enemy, gangs now focus their potential energy on each other instead of letting the *poor righteous teachers* teach them who their true friend is. The mere fact that young and some 'old' Black, Hispanic and Mexican males socially and geographically spate themselves, show and prove that we still suffer from the epidemic of the Willie Lynch plague. Until 'WE' establish the NEED to put aside our colors, unity amongst Black, Hispanic and Mexican men will only be a thing hoped for.

E: Sexuality

In all male facilities, where conjugal visits are prohibited, homosexuality is basically legal. The leave way for homosexuals to freely participate in an institutional restricted activity without penalties causes conflicts between homosexuals and heterosexual males.

Prison officials not only allow homosexuals to do as they please, they treat 'inmates' of that sexual preference better than non-participants. Homosexuals are more likely to be institutional runners (Trustees), i.e., hall workers, kitchen food preps, commissary workers, administration runners, e.g. wardens' trustees.

Homosexuals are also used as informants for institutional officials. This is the 'supposedly' normal ways of prison, and the things that's promoted. Correctional officers make it a comfortable living environment for homosexual, and a place of unease for heterosexual males. To add shame to this effect, prison guards often gawk and whistles at gays in tight fitting clothing, and also bring them female garments. These nefarious actions are the cause of conflicts between homosexuals and heterosexual males— and thus the separation continues.

F: Ethnic and Race Groups

Below the Mason Dixie Line in what was once considered as the "Confederate state of AmeriKKKa", racism is as vivid today as it was doing Post Reconstruction, Jim Crow, and the Civil Rights era combined. The same edicts, laws and social views of these pasted era is displayed today under the disguise of "Industrialized Prisons System". This may not sound familiar, but it viewed from its previously title "Industrialized Slave System", the recollection of a cruel and evil epochal will soon kick in. 'Penitentiaries' are America's new plantations in which citizens (especially Black males) are legally reverted back to slaves, and servitude. Another aspect of criminalizing Black U.S. citizens is "Population Control', or plainly stated, keeping the Niggers in check.

When the issue of racial discrimination or racism within the U.S. judicial system is mentioned, THEY, legislators and executives, always act disavowed, as if it doesn't exist. The most common statements used by these politicians are, "The penal system is made up of men and women of multiracial backgrounds, and we incarcerate white males and females at the same rate as the African-American Justice system." However and whenever, these fallacies are uttered by these 'Poly-trickers'- "I promise to be tough on crime." They're not speaking of crimes in general, what they really mean is, "I promise to lock up more BLACKS, to make White people feel safer." We know they always keep their promises.

In Alabama slave quarters, Blacks outnumber whites 4 to 1, and all other enslaved ethnic groups are estimate 25 to 1. These statistic are often manipulated by enlisting or classifying "others", i.e., Mexicans, Asians and Latinos as white males and females.

Racial riots on these modern day plantations occur without warning. In fact, racial conflicts is the leading cause of most riots that take place within the U.S. mortuaries. The number of senseless deaths caused by these violent disturbances is more than any other penal system in the world. Because America was established on White Supremacy and the plague of racism, its leading advocate, ALABMA, showcase overt racism at every possible opportunity it gets.

In slave holdings, such as William E. Donaldson, formerly West Thomas Jefferson' plantation. An area where convict leasing took place daily. The disarrayment between Black slaves and white inadventurous servants are often instigated by subjugated Negros and Good Ol' Boys hired as correctional officers. The unity between Black Alabama incarcerated citizens and White Alabama incarcerated citizens is feared by the bourgeois elite who profit off this lucrative slave economy. But the grant will wake! And from his slumber WE will scream:

~FREE ALABAMA!

Freedom, it's nonbiased, nonsectarian,

Freedom is anti-hate, anti-oppression

Freedom is optimistic, proactive;

Freedom is for all; and FREE

ALABAMA is a Movement!

G: Religion

The U.S. Constitution or The Grand Law of the land stemmed from the Magna Cara, a charter of liberty for English people and was obtained from King John in 1215 A.D. The Magna Carta marked a decisive step forward in the development of constitutional government. In 1777, the American colonies cut their ties with her mother, Great Britain, and became an independent nation. This was fathered by the first signees of the declaration of the independence on July 4, 1776. Thereafter, the second Continental Congress appointed this document was known as the Articles of Confederation, American's first constitution. (Ratified in 1781).

The so-called Finding Fathers of this government was said to be 'Good Christian People." The law separating church and state was not established yet, and didn't come into existence until 1786-1787, years after the forming of this "FREE" and "INDEPENDENT" country. These same 'Revolutionaries', if you want to call them that, who fought against a tyrant King, were tryannos slave-masters over their African subjects. It was their White Supremacist belief that validate the enslavement of 'Humans', whom they regarded as soulless savages. It was deem that slavery along with 'Christianity" that would civilize these immoral heathens.

Most colonists were deeply religious and made great effort to maintain the virtue of the church. In southern states called the 'Bible Belt', the church still held the grand law in their hands—the Bible. However, the 'RELIGION' of

Christianity was infiltrated by White Supremacist who used the Bible and the church to justify their evil deeds.

Today, Blacks make up the vast majority of the Baptist church. Since the beginning of the 20th century, American has witness a spate of 'Black Mega Churches', with an average of 300 to 2000 members. Looking at it from these numbers, one might say, 'That's Great!" Blacks are finally getting their just due. B-U-T if you do the knowledge from the bottom up, you'll know that this means that because America has an incarcerated rate of 716 people per every 100,000; and because 68% of that 716 are of minority race, Black and Brown males/females ages 19 and older, that three out of every four members in the Black Church has a family member locked up in one of Americas' New Slave Plantation.

Why don't churches contest 'unjust' laws and crooked law makers?

Answer. Because the government gives churches tax breaks and to her leniencies in exchange for noninvolvement in state and government affairs. Also, we must keep in mind that the church was the first judicial system. That's like asking the brother of a slave owner, to aid his brother's slave in escaping, when the brother is befitting from the labor of the slaves his brother own. To prove my contention, history affirms that the first act of 'grand larceny', was commission by the Pope. Also the fact that every patron involved in the criminal act of slavery justified their evolvement and based their participation on religious beliefs.

Nowadays, the church and state still have a 'hand and hand', 'scratch my back, I'll scratch yours' relationship. In most Penitentiaries, like Alabama; if an inmate is granted the privilege of parole, he or she will be 'traded off' to one of the numerous Post Incarceration camps like SIR (Supervised Intensive Release), PDL (Pre-Discretionary Leave), Life Tech Transition center or Halfway House. If giving the basis of the 'programs' by the maker and owners, the said purpose of them would be well accepted. These institutions are supposedly designed to prepare of newly freedman for society. LOL!

The minimum time a person serve before he becomes eligible for the consideration of parole is 5-10 years, most likely the later. So these crafters and grafters would have family members and inmates believe that these programs are for the benefit of the parolee. This is as far away from the truth as Pluto is from the Sun, and that's 3,680,000,000 miles. These 'extended prison camps' are not designed to equip a person with the life skill they need for society. Nor, do they teach or train a person in the field of entrepreneurship which is the one life skill that's proven to beat the odds of recidivism. Instead, the programs promotes and aid in the continuity of the convict leasing system.

What these institutions do prepare a person for is to be a laborer and a consumer, and to compete against lower classed people who have not been marked with the X on their back; in an already failing job market system. What's ironic about the facilities and programs, is that 90% of them are owned and operated by the church or members of it. These systems are slave-makers of the poor, and teach and promote a doctrine similar to the 'suffer and toil while you on Earth and go to Heaven when you die' slave philosophy of antebellum time.

This is not to be taken as a debasement of True Christianity, nor do I hold any ill sentiment towards real Christians. My intended purpose is to express the power that the church have, but choose not to use in the manner in which Jesus would use it, and that is to war against the principalities, against the powers, against the rulers of darkness of this age, against spiritual hosts of wickedness in the heavenly places.

The true followers of Jesus must condemn those who use his name to shield their dirty religion, which is called Christianity. Jesus teachings was not slavery and oppression, it was freedom, justice and equality. Real Christ like disciples must take up the whole armor of God and take church back from the Devil who gives authority to the Beast to devour the original people of the planet Earth.

H: That Mark System

In 1870, the National Prison Association, now called the American Correctional Association (ACA), devised new provisions for jails and prisons called the Declaration of Principles. Under this new system, prisoners were able to gain their freedom by earning *marks*. These points, or *marks* as they were called, was only awarded to a selective few, those whom the system considered trustworthy;

called Trustees. Prisoners worked to gain these *marks*, usually in institutional jobs or on jobs hired by businesses that had financial interest in prison labor.

In the late 1800s and early 1900s, the only people who owned businesses to hire these delinquents were ex-slave owners who still had fields of cotton, rice, tobacco and soy beans to be picked. Also railroad and coal mining companies were in need of real laborers provided by prisoners and 'reverted slaves' according to the 13th Amendment.

Five years after the Civil War, the number of Blacks imprisoned went from 0 to 34%, because this new system was practically legal, these political prisoners were worked extra hard, some until the pint of death.

In a report by Robert Dawson, one of the first Presidents of the Board of Inspectors of Convicts, (the Alabama Division), it revealed that between the years of 1865-1869, the death toll of Black prisoners was 41%. In northern prison where 'Convict Leasing' was not practiced, the death rate was only 1%. Despite the increasing number of deaths, prisons became the next big business for America, and a cash cow for the formal slaveholding states. Private investors quickly invested money into facilities, in exchange for cheap or fee labor.

The use of chain gangs is still practice today in the 21st Century. And if you ever have a chance to witness a 'squad' of prisoners working on the side of public highways, or other state and private sites, you'll understands why THE NEGRO STILL IS NOT FREE.

Inmate work squads are the replicas of antebellum slaves' sets. Although this type of drudgery is not publically called convict leasing, for the same work any other free person would be paid $15-20 for, inmates on these job site only receive *marks* toward their freedom and a peanut butter and jelly sandwich in a brown paper sack.

The billions of "$ $ $" these 21 Century slave owners make off of America's new cash cows (Incarcerate Citizens) is used to operate its carceral system. Just ask who pays the water bill? Who pays the light and the gas bill? Who pays for the outdated food and generic medicine? When you're finish with your paper trail, the road stops at America's first major commodity sold on Wall Street; — SLAVES, BLACK SLAVES!

The system has not changed. Do the math! SLAVE + Labor + Product = a rich ruling class of slave makers. The same *mark* system that is used now is the same system that was used in Pre-Civil War days. The only difference is the wording. Now, you're called a trustee. Back then you were called a 'House Nigger'. Also, it's well known that these slaves that's deemed trustworthy are put in positions to spy on, sedate, oversee, control; and if necessary, kill another slave if he/she obstinately disobey or disrupt the master's system.

It's often said, "A house divided, will not stand." The same goes for incarcerated citizens throughout America. As long as inmates, prisoners, convicts, etc…see their fellow man as his enemy, they'll never know and understand who it is that's really opposing them!

THE ALARM CLOCK HAS RUNG! – WAKE UP!

Inmates that are qualified for these *marks*, usually have minimum sentences or a split sentence. The conflict and separation emerges when an inmate with life or life without, or an inmate with a load of time becomes envious of a 'short timer'. To entrap someone with little time to do a 'lifer' might provoke others in numerous ways, including sexual. Mot times, these incidents result in a violent outcome. For the lifer, it doesn't affect him in any way if he receives a disciplinary or a new case.

On the other hand, the short timer risk his opportunity of retuning back to his family in the shortest time possible, or returning home at all. The only winner in these situation is the prison system. The longer both inmates remain in or on these plantation camps, the more free labor the prison get from them. The more funding the prison receives from local, federal and private entities. Also, that means more dollar signs coming from inmates provided for by their families. More money spent on the commissary, on food and hygiene packages, medical cost and we can't forget about the rent. That's right, I said the rent cost. It's thoroughly known that all plantation camps, over and double, tax its incarcerated citizens for the defected products they sell.

When the topic of 'Slavery' comes up in any conversation, a lot of people, White and Black, become elusive to the subject. Some White people don't like to talk about it because it recollect the evil of their predecessors and make them acknowledge the potential within themselves. A lot of Black people don't like to discuss it because it makes them feel embarrassed and subordinated. This historical fact has gotten so distasteful in the mouths of some, that in 2015 McCraw Hill Education Inc.; the publishing company responsible for printing grade school U.S. History books, downplayed the entire events of the slave trade. Instead of printing the facts, that Africans were kidnapped from their homeland and transported in the bottom of slave ships to American; as slaves. The new books would have read that Africans volunteered as indentured servants to come to the new found land and help develop it. A Texas mother just so happen to read her son's history book and noticed that discrepancies.

Another example is the term 'Diversity' used when referring to forums that are hand selected to talk about racism and race relations. However, as much as some people try to blot out this blood stain deep in Americas' fabric, we are reminded daily, every time a myelinated person is legally lynched in a courtroom and sent to prison.

The beast hasn't changed its intentions, just because it has gotten older and bigger. Its hate and aggressiveness sis till the same, it's just its method of operating has become in cognitive.

During the first centuries of the slave trade, the capturing of young African males and females age 5 to 21 was highly profitable. Where do you think the word 'Kidnapping' come from? Even after the transporting of slaves from Africa was outlawed, the monopolization of slavery always centered itself around the African female and her male off spring. To show and prove this, let's re-examine the whole scheme.

1) History reports that there were more women and children captured and brought to America than men.
2) On the plantation, a scientific breeding process was implemented to ensure long range economic stability through the male child.
3) After 1865, all of the confederate states' constitutions aimed at the under-education and the miss-education of African children.

As I stated before, there is nothing that has changed about the Beast.

When the Black Codes were enacted during the reconstruction years, no Black person was exempt from being arrested; and that's regardless of age and gender. Before the Civil War, there was no need to imprison Black people because for every law, code, ordinance and said to be statue; that was allegedly broken. The trial was public and speedy, the guilty verdict was unanimous, and the sentence was always death. The Black Codes not only kept slavery in this perpetual de jure state, it also opened the doorway for the first wave of Black prisoners. It is documented that the majority of the prisons in the south, such as Kilby Correctional Facility located in Mt. Meigs. Alabama (Montgomery), that the young Black boys were sent there as young as 13 years-of-age.

In the almost 20-years of the 1800s, child labor was very prosperous, mainly because children were paid less than adults. So what would happen is that someone who works for some factory or a company would accuse a child (usually between 10-18 years-old) of a crime, such as stealing. That child would be tried and convicted of whatever made-up-accusation the alleged victim testified to. Then the owner or boss of the company would tell the judge to let the child work for them in order to "pay off his/her debt to society". Even after 1930, when child labor had become illegal; if s/he was duly convicted of a crime, it was still legal to lease him or her out to a company with monetary invested interest in convict labor.

At this moment, you're probably saying that that was in the 1800s and early 1900s, and that times are not like that anymore. Well, as of 2015, U.S. law now allow children age 12 and up to work unlimited hours on farms and for other agricultural companies. There main employee— young Back boys convicted of minor crimes. According to a report conducted by the Sentencing Project, 41 states, along with D.C. area has set the statutory limit for a youth at the age of 16, making it legal for a teenager ag 17 and up to be charge as an adult. In states like Michigan, Texas, South Carolina, Wisconsin; Louisiana, Georgia and Missouri, the age limit is 16. In New York, North Carolina and Alabama, the age that a juvenile can be charge as adult is 15. In 34 states along with the D.C. area, if a child has been sentence as an adult, regardless of their current age s/he will always be charge as an adult.

Imagine this scenario as a 15 year old male gets caught stealing a T-shirt out of store. He gets arrested and instead of going to a juvenile center, he goes to an adult jail. Ding, his court hearing, the judge tells him that his facing 20 years for "larceny", a word which he doesn't know the definition of. Because he lives with just his mother in a low income government housing project, he cannot afford a lawyer. So his appointed attorney by the state convinces him to take a plea bargain for a lesser offense of "theft". He agrees because he's scared, and is sentence to 1 year and 6 days in prison, and 4 years on probation. The youth gets out at age 17 and returns back to high school. Although he has served his time and has left his past behind him, he's still looked upon by his peers as a "criminal"; and therefore he begins to behave in such a manner. Also, even if he completes high school, he will still be barred from getting certain jobs, and will be ineligible to vote or bear arms.

Sounds like this is just a made up story. Despite the past evidence of the governments Counter Intelligence Program, or COINTELPPO, recent information shows that the U.S. government still has a program intact which intact which targets communities with a high concertation of Black and Latinos. The federal government has once again implemented the antagonizing and criminalizing of African and Latino men, in particularly the youth; with such tactics as "Stop and Frisk" "No Saggin Law" (sagging spelled backward is niggas), "aggressive policing in urban communities" and "Control policies i.e., curfews".

Currently, there are 21 states, including the D.C. area, which automatically charge some youth as adults for a set of street drug related crimes. Alabama is one of the five states that automatically charge youth as adults for any street drug related offense. More ever, Black people are more than two and a half times as likely as White people to be arrested and imprison for minor narcotics possession. According to research done by the Sentencing Project, under the subtitle: Lifetime Likelihood Imprisonment of U.S. Residents Born in 2001.

> Statistics shows that 1 out of 17 white men will be incarcerated, 1 in 3 Blacks men and 1 out of 6 Latino men. As for women, studies shows that 1 out of 3 white women will be in jail or imprison, compared to 1 out of every 18 Black women and 1 in 45 Latino women.

This shows and proves that the U.S. Government is still on its fanatic crusade to: "STOP THE RISE OF A BLACK MESSIAH". Since the election of America's first modern-day African-American President, we have witnessed over 30 assassinations of innocent Black civilians. Along with these facts, over 68% of the U.S. prison population are made up of men and women of African and Latino descent.

Between the years of 1991 to 1998, the prison system devoured more youth of color, (ages 14 to 21), than any other years in U.S. history. At its apex, from 1996-97, there were over 12,000 juveniles serving time in adult prisons.

As of 2016, Alabama has about 6,104 citizens serving LWP (Life With Parole), LWOP (Life without Parole) and Virtual life sentences. Out of the 6.104, 66.4% are of African origin, 24.4% of that are people that committed their crime(s) as juveniles.

Another recent study shows that juveniles compared to African Adult males were more likely to receive one of the three sentences; (LWP, LWOP, VLS). As for 'life with parole', juveniles are 49.9% and adults are 42.8%. As for LWOP, juveniles are 63.4% and adults 55.2%. For virtual life sentences (sentences of 50 years or more), juveniles are 64.4% and adults are 51.3%. With overwhelming evidence such as these facts, shortsighted, pro-conservative minded Negroes that willfully disbelieve that there's a conspiracy against diaspora Blacks in these Hells of North America shall remain slaves and a cancer to all Black people.

> "I freed a thousand slaves, I could've freed a thousand more, if only they knew they were slaves." ~Harriet Tubman

The depth of Americas' scorn reaches all the way into the womb of Black women and to their unborn. Just like the ploy of the Willie Lynch system, by creating aggravated circumstance, America can ensure two things. ONE: That teen pregnancy rate is higher amongst Black females; and TWO: that the high school dropout rate is excitedly high for Black males. The ripple effect of this is a young single parent Black female living in a government funded housing project that's infested with all the disadvantages needed to fail, and young Black boys with no education, nor job skills-with only one crucial option and that's the streets and crime. Which only gives them two futures: The grave yard or the prison yard.

This is what Willie Lynch meant by "Interloping Negative". The cycle of failure systematically repeats itself, with only a hand full escaping its grips.

V

S.S. To P.P.: Stop School to Prison Pipeline

A: The Topic of Slavery

The School To Prison Pipeline is an exact replica of the slave catching in the infancy stage of the slave trade. Both entities focused on the African female and her young. The most grievous thing about the School To Prison Pipeline, is that because a lot of people don't see it physically, they don't believe it exist. Therefore they ridicule and shun the poor righteous teachers who try to teach them the "real reality" of the so-called Land of Liberty.

We as people consider child molesters as the lowest of the low and their acts unforgivable sins. Yet, we feed our children to sinister pharmaceutical companies, and Jim Crow schools every day. If we were to consider the long term effects of the child molester and that of the School to Prison Pipeline, we will concluded that the child molester is the lesser of the two evils. A lot of victims, over 80%, that were molested at the young age are able to suppress those memories over time, and live a normal life. As contrary to the S.TO.P.P, once a child is ill labeled, diagnosed and treated for just one of the thousand made-up child behavior disorders, that child will always be chemically depended on depressant and stimulant drugs. And by virtual of this dependency, children, esp., Black males are at a higher risks of becoming addicted to illicit drugs and committing crimes to support their habits.

As discussed earlier, the puffered child behavior ordeal is a billion dollar per year business. Children who have been misidentified as "special, slow, or retarded", by person that's not certified to diagnose that child, i.e., teachers, principals or next door neighbors - those children are three times more likely to drop out of high school than their peers. As for those who's not on the Prozak, Ritalin, etc. just by name calling: "You're so bad…You're just like your father…You slow…You ain't shit…," and on and on. The discouragement is enough to force a child into a life of crime.

Slavery was the main economic streamline for the south. To relinquish that exceptional monetary monopoly, would have not only caused a reversal of the classes, but a complete paradigm shift of the races. No state, whether free or pro-slavery wanted that. So systems were created to ensure the social, political and economic superiority of the ruling class, and these systems are inheritable. You can trace the genealogy of the School to Prison Pipeline all the way back to the Slave Codes of the 1600s.

The core purpose of each system will always remain the same- White superiority and Black inferiority. The man artery which sustain life and growth of each system is the assurance that the children of each generation of the oppressed class remains in the "UN", that means the UN-united, UN-educated, UN-developed and UN-conscious. The saying goes, "When you know better, you suppose to do better." But the Negro doesn't know that he don't know. So he portrays the role of his thoughts. This is why the rich ruling class took over every enterprise in which our five senses and perceive knowledge (light).

They own every major visual broadcasting system, so the only movies, shows, sit-coms and commercials we see are the stereotypical ones – the gangster, the pimp, the bitch, the hoe, the buck dancer, etc... They own every major record distribution system, so the only musical that's promoted is the artists who's singing or rapping about Black hatred, sex, drugs, blood diamonds etc... They own every major food supply system, so the only thing we buy are unwholesome products, can foods, fast foods and junk food. When it comes to our sense of smell, they made sure that every piece of land that's majority populated by Blacks or Latinos are located near factories, and other areas where the air is dangerously polluted. And when it comes to our sense of touch, they go beyond measures to make sure that we believe that everything they make feels better onus; that is why we spend over a billion dollars every year with them.

All of the above mentioned systems play a negative role in the rearing and raising of a child. Just think, how is 90%

of your child's time spent? What kind of music they like or shows they look at? What type of shoes and clothes they wear? How much fast food and junk food they eat? Now ask yourself, who has more influence over your child, the system or you? Do the math, they're at school for eight hours or more, when they're at home; they're playing games, talking on the phone listening to music or watching T.V.

This principle or technique of depreciating the family structure works for the benefit of the macro system. The slave traders and traitors know that 85% of Black people in America is living far below the poverty line, so they promote self-esteem by the attainment of 'Promise Gold' and the glamourizing of the Devils' lifestyle.

In the quest for this fictional materialistic bliss, most Blacks living in colonized settlement choose methods of horizontal violence to achieve this shortsighted goal.

In hood lingo, 'we do what we gotta do to get that paper; from selling crack and weed to selling our children's food stamps off of a EBT card; to robbing and killing our own kind. This vicious cycle is passed down from one generation to the next, the deafer, and dumb and blind we stay, the more the BEAST feeds off our ignorance.

We would think that because it has been 306 years since the Willie Lynch Slave—making methods were introduce to America, that there is no cure for this terminal disease. Contrary to wishful thinking, the antidote has always been available in large quantities. If we were "WHITE WASHED" by and through the processes of menticide, the reversal of this is to develop a "Mentality"; a Black mentality. The cure is to "GO BACK TO AFRICA", mentally. We must resurrect the Mother, see that our mental death was caused by the unconsciousness of our Mother.

In order to stop the STOPP, we must do what the African pledge tells us to do and I phrase:

We <u>must</u> Remember the Humanity,

Glory and Suffering of Our Ancestors

And Honor the Struggle of Our Elders'

We <u>must</u> Strive to bring New Value,

And New Life to Our People;

We <u>must</u> have Peace and Harmony among US.

We <u>must</u> be Loving, Sharing, and Creative.

We <u>must</u> Work, Study, and Listen

So We may Learn;

Learn so We may Teach.

We <u>must</u> Cultivate Self-Reliance.

We <u>must</u> Struggle to Resurrect and Unify Our Homeland;

We <u>must</u> raise many Children for Our Nation;

We <u>must</u> have Discipline, Patience, Devotion and Courage;

We <u>must</u> live as Models

To Provide New Direction for Our People:

We __must__ be Free and Self-Determining:

We Are African People

We Will Win!!!

~Ron Daniels

(SO), (RESO), (REVO), EBEL) – LU –THON

Since the resolving of the economic dispute between the North (Union) and the South (Confederate), resulting in America granting its chattel (slaves; the privilege of lie, liberty, or property. Everyone, literally, everyone has concocted a so-called answer to the 'Negro' problem(s). All kinds of movements, organizations, religions, politicians; profiteers and puppets, all have said— 'I got it!' True, some suggestions have worked for those who have accepted that particular doctrine. However; 'We still have a problem'. If just one Black person out of the millions of Diaspora Africans in these Hells of North America have a problem,

WE ALL GOT A PROBLEM!

It's been three-hundred and six-years since the introduction and contamination of Black people with the grafted pathogen called MENTICIDE. Although a lot of people will admit now that slavery was more psychological than physical, only a handful have ever mentioned this genetic engineered mental disorder. Since it's not recognized as a legitimate disorder (__Post Traumatic Slave Syndrome__), people have rendered all

kinds of miscellaneous remedies. Different organizations
and religions say—'Believe this, think this way, be like
us, follow so and so and our problems will be solved.
Politrickers and Puppets say; stay in your places, work
twice as hard, don't act so ghetto, stop having so many
babies, stop selling our drugs, tell some jokes, sing and
dance, jump, rap or run fast and our problems will go
away'!

Solutions! Resolutions! Revolution! Rebellution!

It's been one hundred-fifty-three-years since the ending of
the ending of the Civil War and still no damn solution.
WHY? In my personal opinion, the reason is that most,
(85%) of melaninated people aren't familiar with this
mental, physical and spiritual disorder, nor can they
identify with the symptoms and effects it cause.

Just imagine what America would be like today if
institutions such as Cheyney University of Pennsylvania,
the oldest Black Institution of higher learning in the
country, (1867) Bowie State University (1865) or
Morehouse (1867) and Fisk University (1866) knew and
taught the scientific and psychological aspect of slaver and
the 'Slavery-making system'.

America would be totally different because that would
have set the groundwork and established a core curriculum
from future generation to learn how to break its faux belief
in White superior and Black inferior chain of bondage. If
today, predominant Black and Latino schools would teach
students from books that were written by people who have
their best interest in mind, I'm willing to guarantee that

the success rate would increase and the poverty and crime rate would decrease. In the Honorable Marcus Mosiah Garvery book, *Message to the People, The course of African Philosophy*, he gives an eleven point system that every predominant Black school should make its students learn by memory. The key point is the 11th one which reads:

> 11. In reading books written by white authors, or whatever kind, be aware of the fact that they are now written for your particular benefit of your race. They always write from their own point of view and only in the interest of their own race.

The nucleus of any nation or race of people is its youth. Knowing this fact, this is why neocolonialist of America has always attack the progress of 'Black Education' because they understand that education is the basis of economics. Sadden, but true, with all of the so-called 'freedoms' we have, Black people in America still have not took control of Black Education. Just because the majority of these schools are located in Black communities, and some bear the names of historical Black figures. The text books and curriculum is still set forth by the other people. A class or a course doesn't equate to having an entire school that's structure around Afrocentric principles.

> 'The tale of the hunt will always glorify the hunter, until the Lion tells his story'. ~ African Proverb

> 'Only a fool would let his enemy educate his children!' ~ Malcom X

The reason Black and Latino children enrolled in PSs (Public Schools) and not meet the national Grade Point Average (GPA) is a because the material they are indoctrinated with all year do not stimulate their inner being (soul). In our original land and state of being, everything we established was centered around spirituality, the principles of GOD, Family and MAAT (Law).

Back then, we understood the importance of incorporating God and the ancestors in the rearing and educating of our children. In this western uncivilization, God and state is two totally separate entities. Just think, who would want to remove God from the daily lives of the people—THE DEVIL!

In recent years, school shooting has been rampant. Also, teen pregnancy, suicide and drop-out rate has increased every year since the sixties. Before integration, Black on Black violence among the youth was uncommon. In Revelation, it speaks about a 'harlot who sits on many waters' (America), and who ever drank of her wine of fornication, partake of her sins. With our culture, we have become promiscuous, a race of people who court our *morals, values,* and *principles* to too many different races, all who surpass us in education and economics.

> *As for My people, children are their oppressors,*
>
> *And women rule over them.*
>
> *O My people! Those who lead you cause you to err,*
>
> *And destroy the way of your paths. ~ ISAIAH 3:12*

History bears witness that the original people of ALKEBULUM (Africa) are the Fathers and Mothers of civilization. However, when we stopped honoring the Creator, and stared giving praises to a Mystery God, our children stopped honoring us. When I say children, what I mean is every nationality that descended from the original Black man and woman.

We must re-mind ourselves of our deep rooted spiritual culture in order to get back to the 'way of our paths'. The age of our renewal of self-begun in 2012, which was in the start of Aquarius age. Also, 2012 is exactly 300 years after Lynch's prediction and it was Obama second term in office. In 2012, we also witnessed numerous assignations of Black men, women and children by people who was sworn to uphold the Law (polices). This, in my most sincere opinion, was the Universe giving us a devoted wake up call, and to consent with this belief, the resolution amongst conscientious Black people in this age is— WOKE!

In our 'awakeness', we must become fully cognitive, focused and proficient to secure our survival in this spiritual/physical war. In THE ART OF WAR by Sun Tzu, he speaks about 'shape':

> "All warfare is based on deception. A skilled general must be master of the complementary arts of simulation and dissimulation; while creating shapes to confuse and delude the enemy, he conceals his true dispositions and ultimate intent'.

In recent years, what we have viewed as 'acts of racism' and 'racist people', are merely *shapes*. These *shapes* are made and puppeteered by an 'unseen' puppeteer who intents are to keep us focusing on the 'act' and the 'actor' instead of the 'screenwriter'.

For example, let's break down the game of chess, since it's based on the stratagem and tactics of war. In chess, you have two opposing forces, usually one 'Black' and the other 'White'. There are eight pawns (minions) lined up in front of a ruling class. These pawns represent late groups who are always disposable and replaceable. However, when we view their acts, we believe that they are the totality of White Supremacy. These pawns are only a façade, and with precise tactics can be eliminated off the board.

Next we have a sub-ruling class or rich slave makers of the poor. The reason I say 'sub' is because even though they play a major role in the enslavement of melaninated people; they are not to be look upon as the 'elite' or 'commander in chief'. This fraction consist of 2 Rooks, 2 Bishops, 2 knights, 1 King, and 1 Queen. Let's say that the rooks represent local law enforcement, city and county political figures and local business. The knights could be state politicians, i.e., mayor, senator, etc… The Bishop, which is the closes to the Queen and King can be the government and the Queen and King are the rich-slave makers who own the technology of enslavement. The Queen, who is the most powerful piece of the board, is like the Boss of these major corporations, and the King is the CEO or the proprietor.

Now chess is a fun game, but it can be quite fierce at times. Victory depends on the person who makes the less mistakes. Defeat can come if you underestimate your opponent or overestimate yourself, which means show signs of arrogance. However, it may be, the game doesn't end until the King is capture—CHECKMATE!

We must return back to the mentality of 'It takes a village to raise a child', or there want be a village in the future; only institutions of slavery to raise our children.

As of 2018, Alabama Department of Corrections, ADOC, now house children as young as 15-years-old in level 5 and 6 security prisons (Supermax). Needless to say, none of the teenagers are Caucasian males. If our children are the future, then we (adults) better do what is necessary to secure an unrestricted life of freedom, Justice and Equality for our offspring. In order to shape our real oppressors, we must deny them access to our money and refuse to take theirs if it compromise our MVP (Morals, Values and Principle's) and dispirited the movement. WE must know and understand that the only reason Black and Brown people in America is living far below the poverty line is because we spend our money with the rich ruling classes.

> '…and the merchants of the earth have become rich through the abundance of her luxury.' ~ Revelation 18:3

The 'displacement' actually means the eviction of poor Black and Brown families. This 'homelessness' is one of the ripple effects caused by mass incarceration via the 13th Amendment. This   is   not   a   debatable   issue.

Intergenerational inequality is based upon just one person within one's own linage becoming a victim of 'racial incarceration' where past meets present.

People always say, 'A house divided want stand. Well, the same is true when it comes to incarcerated African and Latino men. Once the male parent is taken away from the family structure, leaving only the female parent to raise the child and provide financial support, she automatically became a slave to government aid, and falls within the guidelines of the Freedman Law. The only solution to the gentrification of what the 1% ruling class calls URBAND communities is to imitate our Asian cousins who lives in areas called 'China Town' and 'Lil Japan'; and who owns 98% of the market and real estate.

Although Americanizes Capitalism creates a lot of disadvantages and inequalities for us, our biggest hurdle is the Trust Issues caused by the Willie Lynch system.

We trust white people to treat us better than we do our own kind. We trust them with our money, our children and our lives. We trust that their 'Hand-outs and Hand-me-downs' are far better than creating and owning our own.

A good general wins battles and eventually wars by exploiting and capitalizing on his enemy's weaknesses and concealing his own.

In understanding this, we must know that weakness means anything that has been mixed, diluted or tampered with isn't in its original form. The thing that has been mixed, diluted and tampered with and is not its original form is our mind. Our beloved brother Malcom X once said:

> 'When we were stolen and brought to these Hells of North American, we were stripped of everything, we lost our language, we lost our religion and culture; and some of us even lost our Damn minds!'

If something or somebody is weak and its weakness is caused by some external force or external influence, the only way that that thing or person can become strong enough to deaf that outside die-ease, is that the internal self of that thing or person becomes stronger than the outer force.

In Willie Lynch's speech: THE NEGRO MARRIAGE UNIT, he quotes the following to his audience:

> "Our 'experts' warned us about the possibility of this phenomenon occurring, for 'they' say that the mind (of the African) has a strong drive to correct and re-correct itself over a period of time if it can touch some substantial original historical base."

In order to defeat our oppressors. We must correct and re-correct our ways to things. Everything starts with a thought. Gotama Buddha said:

> Mind precedes all phenomena, mind matters most, everything is mind-made. If with an impure mind you speak or act, then suffering follows you as the cartwheel follows the foot of the draft animal.

If with a pure mind you speak or act, then happiness follows you as a shadow that never departs.

B: The African Pledge

The renewal of the mind, or as the Christians say—Born again! We must go back and study what they did to build a Black Wall Street, an African Town and Harlem, NW. There must be a bridge built between the youth and the elders. Love is our only savior. Our enemies has gone to the ends of the earth to ensure that we never return back to the true path of GOD. Even Willie Lynch said this:

> "…and they advised us that the best way to deal with the phenomenon is to shave off the brute's given path."

What does Lynch mean by 'shave off'? The Biblical story of Samson should give us a clear explanation of what 'shave off' refers to. In the story of Samson, he was chosen by God. His mother was told not to drink wine or similar drink, and not to eat any unclean thing; and no razor shall come upon his head, for the child shall be a Nazirite to God from the womb—stop! It's proven by Biblical and historical facts that the ancient Nazarenes where Black people with dread locks.

Now in the story, Samson's hair was his source of strength and his spiritual connection to GOD. How the story is narrated; Samson went to a town called Timnah, which was occupied by Greco-Romans at the time. Samson saw this woman, whom was fair skinned, had long blonde hair and blue eyes (probably a Kardashian), who was the daughter of a Philistine. So Samson, with his jungle fever wanted to marry the woman despite his mother and father disapproval of it. To make a long story short, Delilah tricked Samson into telling her where his strength came from. Although Delilah was married to a Black man she still went against him for her own people. When Samson told her about his hair and him being a Nazarite to God, she hoodwinked him to fall asleep in her lap, then had another man shave off the seven locks of his head. Then she began to torment him, and his strength left him.

Sound like a former LA Lakers' player or a gold player we know. I would say it sounds like the Juice story, but then Delilah and that white man would have been found Dead!

The seven locks on Samson's head represented Divinity, our true nature as Black God's made it the image and likeness of Supreme Black God. The seven locks also mean the knowledge of God and once that knowledge is 'shaved off', we become disconnected from God and from there, we become disconnected with ourselves. This is the reason slave traders shaved the heads of African males either before they left Africa, or once they were in cages in breaking ports.

The Bible is written in two phases, one from a historical aspect, and the other is from a metaphoric/symbolic aspect. The historic is physical, the metaphoric/symbolic is spiritual. In knowing that we can assume that Samson's hair (7 locks) is meant to be interpreted on spiritual level, rather from a mundane viewpoint.

Proof of this is the BLACK POWER MOVEMENT (BPM) of the late 60s and 70s. A time when Black People wore their hair in 'Afros' or Natural' symbolizing there deep spiritual connection to Mother Africa and their true nature. The BPM was a time of equality and peace, also an awakening for many Blacks who were dead in the coherency—Negro! A lot of people hated this 'New and unruly look', especially J. Edgar Hoover and his Cointelpro minions. Only because it represented 'Strength', which is why it is called the BLACK POWER ERA!

Power is truth and force, we know that truth knocks the brain out of falsehood. When we understand the truth about ourselves and our connection with GOD, our enemy's falsehood about us will no longer dictate who we are and our course of living. Their power over us will quickly fade, and we will once again know true liberation. This is what Elijah meant by 'to be born again'.

The slave makers of the poor study us thoroughly, like laboratory scientific experimentations. They study our past, present and future. These Mad Scientist continue daily to come up with new methods to exterminate to free thinking ability of African people in these Northern Hell holes. This system of hate in the Bible identified itself as legion, and said that they were many. In the Willie Lynch speech, he uses the pronouns 'They' and 'Ours' when referring to the experts (scientist), also meaning many.

In the story Jesus found a man who was possessed by these demons. After demanding that they come out of the man, the demons asked could they enter into a herd of swine; and Jesus granted them permission. This story sounds really supernatural, but if look at from its deciphered aspect, it's really understandable.

According to a Biblical concordance, the word legion means Roman soldiers or empire. When you're a soldier for any government, kinship or sovereign, you develop a certain mind frame or mentality. Soldiers are trained to do what they are ordered to do. This man that Jesus encountered had the mind frame of Rome, which made him to appear possessed. So what Jesus did was, he taught him to not to think and act like the Romans. Jesus reproached the mentality of Rome that was driving the man crazy. These demons have many functions and cause people to do many ungodly acts.

In the movie FALLEN starring Denzel Washington, the same demons were able to transfer from one person or thing to another just by touching. These forces of evil can appear in MANY forms such as: Music, Television, Movies, Phones, People and anything that can transmit energy through wavelength. All of these powers can make people think and act a certain way, just like the man who Jesus found possessed. For a more modern example, let's do the science of the music and movies Black American make and love.

In the early 80s when "RAP" was just being born in the days of Kool Here, Whoodini, Scott LA Rock, bog boom boxes, and break dancing, it was all about "Rockin' a party and pop-locking contest. These pioneers were the progenitors of conscious hip hop and paved the way for greats like Rakim, KRS One, Public Enemy, and gangster to name a few. During this era, young and elder Blacks were wearing African medallions Koris and crowns and rocking the RED, BLACK AND GREEN. Rap was hated by the rich rulers because it was rebel they couldn't buy or control. So what these blood suckers of the poor did was took over the distribution of music, which forced most Record labels and independent artist to either sign their life on the dotted line or starve. Owning this major system gave them the power to change the messages written within rap music. This was the introduction of **Gansta** music. Hip hop went from **FIGHT THE POWER, SELF-DESTRUCTION** AND **WE'RE ALL IN THE SAME GANG** to Dope Man. Pimpin' ain't easy, and bangin' on wax.

I've always been an activist for rap and the entire hip hop culture. Growing up in the 80s and 90s, I can attest to both forms of this street poetry. I was break dancing, be-bopping and spray painting every wall I could find. All that changed around 88' or 89', I traded in my Kool Moe Dee crown for an all-black Raiders hat and my King Tut medallion for a gold chain. Doper and Dope Boy music was everywhere, on every corner and in every household in some shape or form.

Some may say that Gansta rap or Reality rap was birth from these conditions, and rapping about it was an avenue of expressing what they saw. No one will ever admit the influence and control White corporate American had over the creativity of the rapper and what got played on the radio. Most rappers were admitted to *"Working with the People"*. But just think about this, rappers was encouraging young Black people to sell crack, gang bang and rob another Black person during a time when America was crusading its *War on Drugs* in Black communities.

That's the same thing as a traitor/informant conspiring with the FEDS to get someone to commit an illegal activity. Rap music had become a form of entrapment for those that didn't know how the system work.

These colonizers did the same thing with Black cinema. We went from watching Shaft stick it to the man, to stereotypical movies depicting Black people as *Drug sellers and users, Pimps and hoes, Gansters, gang members and clowns.*

We can't view the above forms as just entertainment, and ignore the subliminal message propagated by the shatans. No one can deny that the movie "Colors" spread the gang culture of California across America. Cali Bloods and Crips probably would have migrated to other states and cites eventually, but "Colors" made Crips and Bloods overnight. New Jack City had everybody trying to be the next Nino Brown. This is not an attack on anyone in particular, however, if these same directors and actors would have made movies contrast to the Black inferior racial profile that America has always portrayed Blacks as; I truly believe that the state of Black America would be totally different.

"WE ARE MANY", is a statement to think about very deeply. Here's something else to think about, Jesus casted the demons into a herd of swine (pigs), who went mad and dove off a cliff. If the devil taught us to eat the wrong food (swine), which made us mad-people who don't know the ledge of the devil's system, so we fall off the edge into their uncilivation, **Why do we still eat off the master's table?**

They say insanity is doing the same thing twice, and expecting different results. We tried these same devils before to provide us with food, clothing, shelter and equality, but we got nothing but welfare, unemployment, gentrification and discrimination, and is shot down by the same ones who advocate this '**We The People**' doctrine. When are we going to come to the conclusion that '**Providing for self**' is a literal term? That's not a co-dependent of the people that's depending on us to make them rich. Our next move got to be our best move. The game of Chess teaches you strategic thinking, and also how to implement a plan tactically, so we must stop thinking emotionally. Living by our feelings.

Every borough, neighborhood, ghetto etc, that's densely populated with African and Latino people need to start having community meetings at least twice a month. These town-house meetings need to be structure like 'Think Tanks'. At every meeting, education and economics need to be the two main issues, because these two factors will re-duce crime and bring unity, love and stability back into the "Hoods".

Now when it comes to giving up money, we tend to be very hesitant, and down right against giving another Black person our money. The Willie Lynch distrust sentiments kick in real fast when the words 'give' and 'money' is in the same sentence. But think about this, we put money in the collection plate with the notion of paying tithe to God who really don't accept worldly briberies from someone who just want to come into his Kingdom. Jesus said, *"Render therefore unto Caesar the things which are*

*Caesar's; and unto God the things that are God's." ~ St.
Matthew 22:17-21*

We have no complex going to these high price department
stores and spending hundreds to thousands of dollars on
outfits to wear to nightclubs. We really need to regulate
our priorities better, we spend more money on weed,
liquor and bullshit than we do preparing a future for
ourselves and our children. Most of us will only contribute
at the point of a sword or on the fucked end of a gun. If a
person doesn't give freely with the good intention of the
betterment for Black people, then, them nor their money
should be welcome into the community. Survival of Black
people is a million times more valuable than friendship.
This is why other races excel far greater than the Negro of
North America, because they don't separate themselves
from the whole.

If a Mexican or Asian come to America and start making
money, they send money back to their families and
community members to do the same. The next thing you
know you have an entire neighborhood of Mexican or
Asians as diaspora Africans, we must stop letting
Caesars's money divide us. A community is family,
regardless of what three you're from, we're all the sons
and daughters of one mother and one father. Community
controlled. I can't stress the importance enough of owning
and controlling the 'Hoods' we call ours.

In the sixties, we had the 'Protest to Progress Strategy'.
Where we couldn't go, we went there until they invited us.
Where we couldn't sit down, we sat in some places, and
stopped sitting in others until they gave us a seat. We

protested their businesses until we progressed in their establishments. That was the sixties, and although we can borrow some tactics from the Civil Rights Movement; we must develop all new plans to succeed in this war. Instead of wanting a seat at their tables, we got to put our minds and money together and buy the house to put the table in. According to certain religious there, if you discover the name of the demon, then you can cast him out of whomever he or they possesses.

Willie Lynch was just a spokesperson for the legion, that's why he never revealed the names of the "**Our**" and "**They**". As I said earlier, the only way to shape the arch devil is to disrupt their flow of economics. If you want to find out how someone really feels about you, start getting money without them, and when they try to borrow some; don't lend it to them. The response will be instant hate and a lot of harsh words. Now this is where we must be expertly strategic, and not to expose our left hand, for we know that the devils are infamous murders of aboriginal people (Black, Brown, Red and Yellow).

This is not a mission impossible, nor is this a book to read and then just throw it on a shelf. We must take that initiative in this day and age. For this is the age of enlightment but it's also the age of mass incarceration of African and Latino men. The saying goes: There's nothing new under the sun, so this is not a new occurrence. Black and Brown men are being snatched up out of our communities just like they were being snatched out of villages in Africa and South America. The 'Privatization' of prison by Slave Trade Investors is a major field for the

Mass Incarceration and the School to Prison Pipeline systems. The list of businesses is the vast to compile in one book, but products such as Coke, Snicker candy bar, Coast soap, and all major brand Tobacco cigarettes come from rich slave trade investors. Incarcerated citizens spend over a billion dollars yearly on these products and more, and that's not including the free labor we provide, which amounts to about half a billion along.

This is why the Devil want let the Negro go free, because the Negro is a wealth building commodity. But if the Negro cease being a Negro, cease being a slave for American slave owners, and start being himself, then the market value on the Negro would default and the whole system will crash. If the Negro becomes an 'African', with all the morals, values and principles and the Black Pride of Pen, Africanism, then we'll really see a 'Great Depression', because these rich slave owners of the poor would become so worried and hoary headed; they just might start killing themselves and everyone they see.

Truth needs no helper or anyone to testify on its behalf. It stands along and fearless, not wavering nor inconsistent in its speech or action. Our truth can only be known once we become independent of our slave owner's money. Remember, if money is the root of all evil, and the Devil is the chief conductor of evil, then when we 'chase that money and stack them racks', who do we work for?

There's an old Blues legend about Robert Johnson, and how he sold his soul to the Devil at a cross-road to become the greatest guitar player ever. Nowadays, it seem as if every direction the Negro turn, he's standing in the midst of a cross-roads, looking into a trader's eyes who's promising him gold for his labor, more than they are earning in his own country. The contract was signed with blood, the agreement was that Robert Johnson send as many souls to hell with his music as he can. Robert Johnson sold out a lot of Black people, and the Negro today is still selling Black people out just for the Devil's promised gold.

The title of this book comes from a chorus in a Ghetto Boys song called 'NO SELL OUT'; which echoes: The Negro, The Negro, The Negro, Still is not Free—No Sell Out!

Askari Hesabu

Commonly known as Mathematics, is a political activist and a member of the grassroot organization, FREE ALABAMA MOVEMENT. Growing up in Birmingham, Al., and living one block away from the 16th Street Baptist Church, he grew up hearing countless stories about the Civil Rights era. Falling victim to the same system that persecuted his fore parents, Hesabu then known as, Bryant Evans, was incarcerated in the mid 90's. Some may say that his incarceration was due to his participation in the gang and drug culture that plundered his community, and the entire inner city of Birmingham, however, Hesabu found out that his incarceration was due to his lack of knowledge of the BEAST. This book is a must read for everyone who has felt the oppression of the BEAST. For those with incarcerated love ones held against their will in one of AmeriKKKa's new slave plantation, this book is a light in their darkness.

REMEMBER THE CIVIL WAR WAS WON WITH PHICICAL WARFARE, NOW WE MUST FIGHT SPIRITUALLY AND POLITICALLY TO STOP THE S.TO.P.P AND MASS INCARCERATION!

REFERENCES

The Willie Lynch Letter
Alabama History Past and Present
Supreme Wisdom Booklet by Elijah Muhammad
Quote by Noble Drew Ali
Quote by Patrick Henry
Alabama Civil Action Case: John F. Knight Jr. et al, Vs.
The state of Alabama, et al;
Quote by President Abe. Lincoln
Quote by Kenneth Stampp
Quote by W.E.B. Du Bois
Plessy vs. Ferguson
Brown vs. Board of Education of Topeka
Quote by Frederick Douglas
Quote by El Hass Malik El Shabazz
Quote by Thomas Heflin
Quote by John Rogers
Almanac (2009 – 13)
Blacks Law Dictionary
Quote by Malcolm X
The Blueprint by Roderick L. Emery
Quote by Malcolm X
Discipline and Punish by Michel Foucault
National Institute of Correction
U.S. Census Bureau
Center on Budget and Policy Priorities
A.D.O.C. Reports on Inmates Violence
The National Registry of Exonerations
ALA. Rules of Court
Prison Legal News
Sentencing Project
African Pledge Note: The word 'will' was replaced with
'must' to show a sense of urgency. Ron Daniel

---

[i] file://Y:\BPP_Books\temp\Fw It is never too late to get up off of your knees and fight for w... 8/20/2005

[ii] file://Y:\BPP_Books\temp\Fw It is never too late to get up off of your knees and fight for w... 8/20/2005
https://ia800503.us.archive.org/31/items/WillieLynchLetter1712/the_willie_lynch_letter_the_making_of_a_slave_1712.pdf
http://www.itsabouttimebpp.com/BPP_Books/pdf/The_Willie_Lynch_Letter_The_Making_Of_A_Slave!.pdf

[iii] Dictionary.com http://www.dictionary.com/browse/racism

[iv] (https://www.waywordradio.org/word-not-crystal/)

[v]
https://www.google.com/search?rlz=1C1RNLG_enUS685US685&biw=1440&bih=745&tbm=isch&sa=1&ei=o5hoW-TeOsnSsAXCq6vICA&q=jim+Crow+began+1890+Wm.+H+Wests+Big&oq=jim+Crow+began+1890+Wm.+H+Wests+Big&gs_l=img.3...18937.25593.0.25969.16.16.0.0.0.0.197.1451.15j1.16.0....0...1c.1.64.img..0.0.0....0.lLlTCYG_3Tk#imgrc=WOYXmI-JQo-DeM: Plus words...

[vi] (https://www.merriam-webster.com/dictionary/inferiority%20complex)

[vii]
https://www.biblegateway.com/passage/?search=Revelation+6%3A8&version=KJV

[viii] tps://www.dictionary.com/browse/pale

[ix] https://www.merriam-webster.com/dictionary/death?utm_campaign=sd&utm_medium=serp&utm_source=jsonld

[x] https://www.merriam-webster.com/dictionary/power